THEORY OF
THERMALLY INDUCED
GAS PHASE REACTIONS

THEORY OF THERMALLY INDUCED GAS PHASE REACTIONS

E. E. NIKITIN

Institute of Chemical Physics,
Academy of Sciences of the U.S.S.R.

TRANSLATED BY SCRIPTA TECHNICA, INC.

TRANSLATION EDITOR, E. W. SCHLAG
Department of Chemistry, Northwestern University

1966
INDIANA UNIVERSITY PRESS
BLOOMINGTON & LONDON

Originally published as:
*Sovremennyye Teorii Termicheskogo Raspada i Isomerizatsii
Molekul v Gazovoy Faze*
by: Nauka Press, Moscow, 1964

Library of Congress Catalog Number 66-12733
Manufactured in the United States of America

TRANSLATION EDITOR'S PREFACE

In recent years a large impetus has been given to the attempt to understand processes in Chemical Kinetics from a microscopic molecular viewpoint. The theories and methods obtained from such a detailed molecular approach are then, one hopes, related to some experimental kinetic observable and through this some order should emerge in our understanding of those molecular processes that eventually lead to the structural changes loosely termed reaction. This book presents a review, and extensions of, current theories of thermally induced reactions, but much of the conceptual method developed here will also be applicable to many of the theories related to photochemistry, energy transfer, reactions in a mass spectrometer, etc. The mountain of theoretical work in Reaction Kinetics has been growing much like that of experimental work, and so it is to be welcomed when one of the major contributors pauses to summarize the current status in an area. Although this book is not completely exhaustive in the area of theoretical reaction kinetics, it represents a valuable summary introduction to research workers in this rapidly expanding field.

EDWARD W. SCHLAG

EVANSTON, JANUARY 1966

CONTENTS

TRANSLATION EDITOR'S PREFACE   v

FOREWORD   ix

**CHAPTER I. THE CLASSICAL THEORY OF UNIMOLECULAR RE-
ACTIONS**   1

1. Thermal Decomposition and Isomerization of Molecules as Unimolecular Reactions   1
2. Variation of Reaction Rate Constant with Pressure. Mechanism
   of Strong Activating Collisions   6
3. Kassel's Model   9
4. Slater's Model   12
5. Effect of Anharmonicity on Reaction Rate   16
6. Anomalously High Pre-Exponential Factors for Rates of Ther-
   mally-Induced Unimolecular Reactions   19

**CHAPTER II. THE QUANTUM THEORY OF UNIMOLECULAR RE-
ACTIONS**   25

7. Kassel's Model   26
8. Slater's Model   41
9. The Quasi-Equilibrium Theory of Unimolecular Reactions   45
10. The Effect of Various Degrees of Freedom on the Rate of Spon-
    taneous Decomposition   60
11. Nonadiabatic Reactions   65
12. Comparison of Theory with Experiment   74

**CHAPTER III. THERMAL DECOMPOSITION OF DIATOMIC MOLE-
CULES**   81

13. The Equilibrium Theory of Decomposition   81
14. A Qualitative Study of the Mechanism of Vibrational Excitation
    of Diatomic Molecules   87
15. Nonadiabatic Transitions between Electronic States of the Dis-
    sociating Molecule   90

CONTENTS

16. Rotation of the Dissociating Molecule   95
17. Model Calculations of the Dissociation Rate   101
18. The Nonequilibrium Distribution Function   118

CHAPTER IV. THE DIFFUSIONAL THEORY OF CHEMICAL RE-
    ACTIONS   129

19. The Classical Theory   129
20. The Quantum Model   138

REFERENCES   147

INDEX   153

FOREWORD

Recent years have seen the appearance of a large number of papers devoted to the theory of thermal decomposition and isomerization of various molecules. This flood of literature is largely the byproduct of attempts to interpret data derived from gas-phase experiments on the kinetics of nonequilibrium reactions. These recent experiments employ new techniques such as flash photolysis, spectroscopic study of reactions, chemical activation of reactants and mass-spectroscopic study of reactions. These new techniques yielded data which do not lend themselves to interpretation within the framework of the Hinshelwood-Kassel theories, which have previously dominated the field. While we are thus faced with new problems, we have for the first time the opportunity to obtain a deeper insight into the intra- and intermolecular processes involved in the transfer of energy. We are also in a position to verify our previous hypotheses on the reaction mechanisms involved. These opportunities have opened up because we now have at our disposal a wealth of accumulated experimental data, a much more mature theory and last, but not least, modern computers capable of calculating the simple models postulated by the theory. The computers render invaluable service, for without them it would be impossible to evaluate all the complex factors involved in the calculation of the rate of a chemical reaction.

In connection with the above, it seemed useful to analyze the reactions of poly- and diatomic molecules from a single point of view, and this despite the fact that, kinetically, the decompositions of the diatomic molecules differ substantially from the decompositions and isomerizations of the polyatomic species. Nevertheless, the two sets of reactions have much in common. In particular, activation plays an important role in both cases, with the specifics of the activation mechanism determining the rate of decomposition of diatomic molecules at all pressures and the rates of reactions of polyatomic molecules at low pressures.

This book discusses the data which have appeared in the literature prior to 1964. However, the reference to experimental work was necessary only for the purpose of illustrating the theory.

I wish to express my gratitude to Academician V. N. Kondratyev and to Prof. N. D. Sokolov, both of whom have read the manuscript and have suggested a number of valuable changes.

E. E. NIKITIN

THEORY OF
THERMALLY INDUCED
GAS PHASE REACTIONS

Chapter I

THE CLASSICAL THEORY OF UNIMOLECULAR
REACTIONS

1. THERMAL DECOMPOSITION AND ISOMERIZATION
OF MOLECULES AS UNIMOLECULAR REACTIONS

The term "unimolecular" is usually applied to reactions which result in a structural change of single molecules or ions. Typical examples of such reactions are the decomposition and isomerization of polyatomic molecules. Correspondingly, the decomposition of diatomic molecules may also be considered to be a unimolecular reaction in a certain limit, although such decomposition is usually treated as bimolecular. This is partly due to the fact that the process of activation as the result of binary collisions is of particular importance in the decomposition reactions of diatomic molecules (by comparison with the decomposition of polyatomic molecules) and it is for this reason that the theory of the thermal dissociation of diatomic molecules has been considered separately (Sections 13-18) from the general theory of unimolecular reactions. Decomposition reactions of diatomic molecules are also classed as bimolecular because they are limited by a second-order collision process. Since, however, the reactions of polyatomic molecules are similarly determined by second-order collision processes under certain conditions, such a formal separation of the reactions of diatomic molecules is not justified. Thus unimolecular reactions (in the above sense) can be kinetically first or second order, depending upon the pressure. Moreover, for molecules containing more than two atoms there is a transitional pressure range in which the order is intermediate, depending on the pressure of the system, and hence it is not meaningful under these conditions to speak of a definite order of reaction.

According to current concepts (see, for example, [7]) unimolecular processes proceed at an appreciable rate only in the case when the molecules of the reactant have an internal energy greater than a certain threshold value E_0. The latter is also known as the critical energy and corresponds to the activation energy for reactant molecules in thermal equilibrium. Such molecules are called *active molecules*. They are produced either in the process of chemical reaction as a result of inelastic molecular collision, or by the impact of electrons, photoexcitation, etc. It should be emphasized that the above concept was developed before tunnel effect reactions were discovered. For such reactions there is no sharp energy boundary separating the nonactive molecules from the active molecules since nonactive molecules still have a certain probability of undergoing unimolecular reaction from their nonactive states. In many cases, however, the correction which must be made for the tunnel effect is small and the earlier treatment can be retained. Reactions in which the tunnel effect is important will be considered separately.

The concept of the *activated molecule* or *transition complex* must also be introduced. This concept arises from a consideration of reactions in the multidimensional configuration space which represents the coordinates of all the atoms in the molecule. The conditions for reaction can be formulated as the condition necessary for the representative point to cross a surface in configuration space which separates the reactants from the reaction products (this surface is known as the critical surface). An activated molecule is that state of an active molecule for which the representative point lies on the critical surface. The activated molecule defined in this way is identical to the transition complex in Eyring's theory of unimolecular reactions [2]. The definition is meaningful only for a classical or, with certain amendments, a quasi-classical description of intramolecular motion. In some cases, the internal coordinates of the activated molecule must be known in addition to the corresponding momenta in order to calculate the reaction rates. It is then necessary to replace the configuration space by phase space in which the critical surface is similarly defined.

The thermal decomposition of a polyatomic molecule in an atmosphere of an inert gas M by the reaction scheme AB → A + B can be used to make clear the individual importance of intramolecular and intermolecular energy transfer in unimolecular reactions. It will be assumed that only binary collisions between AB and M are responsible for the activation of the molecules AB. At sufficiently high pressures the rate of intermolecular energy exchange between AB and M will exceed the rate of intramolecular energy transfer between various parts of the molecules AB. Therefore, details of intramolecular energy transfer will be of secondary importance, and the rate of decomposition will depend only on the nature of the equilibrium energy distribution of the molecules AB. At very low pressures, however, the rate of decomposition is determined by the rate of activation of AB by collision with M, and this will be affected only by the most general characteristics of intramolecular interaction (for example, the density of the vibrational energy states). Thus, in this case also the rate of decomposition is not determined by the details of intramolecular energy transfer. Conversely, in the case of reactions with an extremely nonequilibrium initial distribution, produced in some chemical process by electronic or ionic collisions, it is quite probable that a correlation will exist between the lifetime of the active molecule and its initial state after excitation [121].

Landau's Statistical Theory. As a result of the comparatively slight dependence of the rate of unimolecular thermal decomposition on the details of intramolecular energy transfer it is possible to explain some of the general characteristics of such processes on the basis of a statistical theory. This theory, which was first proposed in a general form by Landau [86], is based on the assumption that the decomposition of molecules occurs as the result of a random redistribution of the internal energy E and of the concentration of a certain fraction of this energy E_0 in one bond of the molecule.* Treating the molecule as a closed system during the period between collisions, Landau used thermodynamic fluctuation theory to determine the probability W of the formation of an activated molecule. This probability can be expressed in the form

$$W \approx \exp\left[(S(E, E_0) - S(E))/k\right], \tag{1.1}$$

where $S(E)$ is the entropy of the active molecule. If the entropy contribution of the reaction coordinate is neglected, then, for a

---

*Ed. Note: A similar concept is at the heart of the Rice–Ramsperger–Kassel theory [6].

sufficiently large number of degrees of freedom, the entropy of the activated molecule can be expressed as $S(E, E_0) = S(E - E_0)$. The rate of spontaneous unimolecular reaction can then be written in the form

$$\kappa(E) = A \exp\left[\frac{S(E - E_0) - S(E)}{k}\right], \tag{1.2}$$

where A is a frequency factor which characterizes the frequency of intramolecular motion. Consideration of the competing reactions of deactivation and decomposition leads to the conclusion that at high pressures the average energy of the molecules which decompose per unit time exceeds the activation energy by an amount equal to the mean energy of one molecule; the rate constant for such molecules can be expressed in the form

$$\kappa_\infty = A \exp(-E_0/kT). \tag{1.3}$$

At low pressures the main term contributing to the decomposition rate is due to molecules with total energy close to the energy of activation, and the rate constant for these molecules is

$$\kappa_0 = Z \exp[S(E_0)/k] \exp[-(E_0 - \bar{E})/kT], \tag{1.4}$$

where Z is the number of collisions per unit time which cause deactivation; $\bar{E}$ is the mean vibrational energy per molecule of the molecules that react per unit time.

The majority of theories of unimolecular decomposition considered below are based to some extent on statistical models which make it possible to evaluate explicitly the frequency factor A and the entropy term and also to derive the number of effective collisions.

2. VARIATION OF REACTION RATE CONSTANT WITH PRESSURE. MECHANISM OF STRONG ACTIVATING COLLISIONS

In order to demonstrate the basic assumptions of the theory of unimolecular reactions the expression for the rate constant κ will be derived within the framework of the method due to Lindemann. It is assumed that the partial rate of decomposition from a state i, which is characterized by a set of coordinates q_i and momenta p_i, is equal to the rate of activation to that state $P(i)$ multiplied by the probability that decomposition will occur within a time $\tau(i)$ such that the molecule does not undergo a deactivating collision within that time. Kinetic equations can be written for the processes of activation and deactivation; these equations are, of course, based on the assumption of the randomness of the collisions. Strictly speaking, analogous equations cannot be written for intramolecular energy transfer since this process is known (for example, for small molecules) to be nonrandom. Therefore, in deriving an expression for κ the method proposed by Slater [130] and developed by Thiele [140] will be used.*

Let Z_{ij} denote the number of collisions which cause the molecule to change from the state i to any other state j. One of the fundamental assumptions of the theory is that Z_{ij} is independent of i; this is known as the strong-collision assumption.† In accordance with the principle of detailed balance, the rate of activation to the state i can be expressed as**

$$P(i) = \frac{Z}{F} \exp\left[-\beta H(p_i, q_i)\right]; \quad \beta = 1/kT, \quad (2.1)$$

where $H(p_i, q_i)$ is the Hamiltonian of the molecule and F is the phase integral. The probability that the molecule will not undergo

---

*An analogous method for photochemical reactions was investigated by Wilson [154].
†Ed. Note: The strong-collision assumption in addition is often also defined to include the assumption that the initial distribution in (p_j, q_j) is in equilibrium.
**Where $Z = \sum_j Z_{ij}$

a deactivating collision during a time τ is

$$P(\tau) = \exp[-Z\tau], \qquad (2.2)$$

and thus the reaction rate constant is given by

$$\kappa = Z \int \exp[-Z\tau(i)] \exp[-\beta H(p_i, q_i)] \frac{d\omega_i}{F}, \qquad (2.3)$$

where F is the molecular partition function and $d\omega_i$ is a volume element in the phase space p_i, q_i. Consider a trajectory leading to reaction on the constant-energy surface of an active molecule, $H(p_i, q_i)=E_0$. Since the molecule is a closed system between collisions, motion along the trajectory in the reverse direction (that is, changing the sign of the time) also leads to intersection with the critical surface which separates the region of reaction products from the region of the reactants. The part of the trajectory which is significant for deactivation corresponds to molecules for which the reaction is not complete; it is over these molecular states that the integration in Eq. (2.3) is carried out. An element of the hypersurface ds can be expressed in the form $d\psi d\sigma$, where $d\psi$ is an elementary time interval between two points moving along the trajectory and $d\sigma$ is an element of the hypersurface normal to the trajectory and with one dimension less than ds. Since the interval $d\psi$ remains constant along the trajectory and the element of hypervolume $d\omega$ is, by Liouville's theorem, conserved, $d\sigma$ must also remain constant. Therefore $d\omega = dEd\psi d\sigma$ in Eq. (2.3) may be replaced by $dEd\psi d\sigma^*$, where $d\sigma^*$ is the element of the hypersurface at the point where the trajectory intersects the critical surface. If τ^* denotes the total time during which the representative point moves along the trajectory in the region of phase space corresponding to molecules for which the reaction is not complete, it may obviously be assumed that $\tau(i) = \tau^* - \psi$. In this expression τ^* depends only on the parameters of the trajectory at the point of its intersection with the critical surface. Thus, integration with respect to $d\psi$ is easily performed and we obtain

$$\kappa = \int_{E_0}^{\infty} \langle 1 - \exp(-Z\tau^*) \rangle \exp(-\beta E) \, dE / F, \qquad (2.4)$$

where $\langle \cdots \rangle$ denotes averaging over $d\sigma^*$:

$$\langle \ldots \rangle = \frac{1}{\sigma^*} \int (\ldots) \, d\sigma^*; \quad \sigma^* = \int d\sigma^*. \qquad (2.5)$$

The element $d\sigma^*$ may be interpreted as the projection of an element of the critical surface on a plane perpendicular to the trajectory. From Eqs. (2.4) and (2.5) the following expressions are obtained for the reaction rate constants at high and low pressures:

$$\kappa_{\infty} = \int_{E_0}^{\infty} \frac{\sigma^*}{F} \exp(-\beta E) \, dE, \qquad (2.6)$$

$$\kappa_0 = Z \int_{E_0}^{\infty} \langle \tau \rangle \frac{\sigma^*}{F} \exp(-\beta E) \, dE. \qquad (2.7)$$

Equation (2.6) is valid when the mean rate of decomposition is small in comparison with the rate of deactivation ($Z\langle \tau \rangle \gg 1$); Eq. (2.7) is valid when the mean lifetime is small in comparison with the time between collisions ($Z\langle \tau \rangle \ll 1$). It will be seen that the reaction rates in the limiting cases of high and low pressures are determined by very general properties of the molecules: the magnitude of the "projection" of the critical surface and the mean lifetime of the active molecules. In the intermediate case the function $1 - \exp(-Z\tau^*)$ must be averaged, which in principle can be done if the trajectory is known. It may take the form of averaging over a lifetime τ^* with a distribution function $h(\tau^*, E)$. In the simplest case it might be assumed that the lifetimes are randomly distributed about a certain mean value $1/\kappa(E)$, so that the distribution function h takes the form

$$h = \kappa(E) \exp[-\tau\kappa(E)]. \tag{2.8}$$

Substituting Eq. (2.8) into (2.4) gives the following expression for the rate constant of a unimolecular reaction:

$$\kappa = \frac{1}{F} \int_{E_0}^{\infty} \frac{Z_3^*}{\kappa(E) + Z} \exp(-\beta E)\, dE. \tag{2.9}$$

The majority of theories of unimolecular reactions which accept the strong-collision hypothesis are based to some extent on Eq. (2.9). A rigorous derivation of the distribution function is obviously an extremely complex problem which can only be solved for the simplest models. In the case of a single harmonic oscillator with a critical surface of the form $q = q_0$ (i.e., reaction occurs when the vibrational coordinate q attains a critical length q_0) the distribution function is not exponential [49, 130]. The distribution function for the case of two coupled harmonic oscillators with a critical surface of the same type has been investigated by Slater [130]. Finally, Thiele [141] and Bunker [52] have calculated the distribution function for the case of two coupled anharmonic oscillators (see below).

3. KASSEL'S MODEL

Kassel's theory is based on the assumptions of strong collisions and the random nature of the redistribution of energy between the degrees of freedom of a molecule, which is represented by a system of harmonic oscillators in the active or activated states. The second assumption involves an implicit allowance for anharmonicity, which enables the interaction between the critical oscillator and the other degrees of freedom. It is assumed that reaction occurs when energy exceeding a critical value E_0 is concentrated in one critical oscillator which then leads to a motion along the reaction coordinate. The probability of such a fluctuation may be expressed in the form

$$W(E, E_0) = g^*(E, E_0)/g(E), \qquad (3.1)$$

where g and g^* are the statistical weights of the active and activated molecules, respectively. Since for a system of s classical oscillators $g_s(E) = E^{s-1}/(s-1)!$, where the units of E are in multiples of $h\nu$ (ν being the fundamental oscillator frequency), g_s^* is given by

$$g_s^*(E, E_0) = \int_{E_0}^{E} g_{s-1}(E - E_0)\,dE = (E - E_0)^{s-1}/(s-1)!, \qquad (3.2)$$

and it follows that

$$W(E, E_0) = [(E - E_0)/E]^{s-1}. \qquad (3.3)$$

An explicit form of the frequency factor $\tilde{\nu}$ can be obtained by assuming the form of the trajectories which lead to the reaction (since σ^* depends on these trajectories). In particular, by assuming that the activated state corresponds to some definite value of the reaction coordinate and that the remaining degrees of freedom correspond to arbitrary values of the coordinate, Giddings [65] showed that the frequency factor $\tilde{\nu}$ is given by

$$\tilde{\nu} = \prod_i \nu_i^* \Big/ \prod_i \nu_i, \qquad (3.4)$$

where ν_i, ν_i^* are the frequencies of the molecule and of the activated complex, respectively (in accordance with the above assumption, the frequencies v_i^* are the frequencies of AB for a fixed value of the reaction coordinate of q_0). Since the number of vibrational frequencies for the activated molecule is one less than the number for the active molecule, the ratio of the products of the frequencies in Eq. (3.4) must be of the order of the frequency of oscillation of the molecule. However, for those cases in which the trajectory in phase space cannot be even approximately described by the superposition of harmonic oscillators, the frequency factor may considerably exceed the "usual" value of 10^{13}–10^{14} sec^{-1} (this will be discussed further in Section 6).

The rate constant at high pressures can easily be evaluated by introducing a rate constant $\kappa(E)$ which depends only on the total energy of the active molecule. On the basis of Eqs. (3.3) and (3.4) the following expression for $\kappa(E)$ is obtained:

$$\kappa(E) = 1/\langle \tau(E) \rangle = \tilde{v} \left(\frac{E - E_0}{E} \right)^{s-1}. \qquad (3.5)$$

The rate constant κ_∞ can then be obviously expressed in the form

$$\kappa_\infty = \int_{E_0}^{\infty} \kappa(E)\, g_s(E) \exp(-\beta E) \beta^s dE = \tilde{v} \exp(-\beta E_0). \qquad (3.6)$$

Comparison of Eqs. (2.6), (2.7) and (3.6) shows that when $\beta E_0 \gg s$

$$\kappa_0 = Z\, [(\beta E_0)^{s-1}/(s-1)!] \exp(-\beta E_0). \qquad (3.7)$$

For intermediate pressures the following expression for the reduced rate constant κ/κ_∞ can be derived from Eqs. (3.6) and (3.7):

$$\frac{\kappa}{\kappa_\infty} = \frac{1}{(s-1)!} \int_0^{\infty} \frac{x^{s-1} \exp(-x)\, dx}{1 + (\tilde{v}/Z)\, [x/(x+b)]^{s-1}} ; \quad b = \beta E_0. \qquad (3.8)$$

4. SLATER'S MODEL

Slater's theory [130] also starts with the assumption of strong deactivating collisions but differs from Kassel's theory in that it is not statistical. It is assumed here that a reaction occurs when an intramolecular coordinate q attains a value q_0 and that the potential energy of the molecule can be expressed as a quadratic function of the displacement of the nuclei from the equilibrium position. Slater's theory explicitly takes into account the interaction of the reaction coordinate with the other degrees of freedom of the active molecule, since q is expressed in the form of a linear function of the normal coordinates Q_i. The value of q_0 is uniquely related to the threshold energy E_0, which is equal to the minimum sum of the energies of the normal coordinates ε_i under the condition that the representative point passes through the critical surface. It is indeed the possibility of introducing noninteracting normal coordinates which violates the condition of ergodicity of the system and makes it impossible to use a statistical model. Nevertheless, both Slater's theory and Kassel's statistical theory for a system of harmonic oscillators must give identical results for the decomposition rate constant at high pressures. This follows because Eq. (2.6) is applicable to both theories and because the critical surfaces are in both theories identical. As was noted above, differences in the mechanism of intramolecular energy redistribution have no effect at high pressures. Thus, Eq. (3.6) for κ_∞ is also valid for Slater's theory.

However, the theories of Slater and Kassel give different results at lower pressures when the mechanism of intramolecular energy transfer becomes important. Since the rate of decomposition at low pressures is determined by the mean lifetime $\langle \tau \rangle$, it is necessary to investigate the time dependence of the reaction coordinate q. The latter can be expressed in the form of a linear combination of the normal coordinates:

$$q = \sum q_i Q_i(t) = \sum_i \alpha_i \sqrt{\varepsilon_i} \cos(\omega_i t + \psi_i), \qquad (4.1)$$

where α_i are the so-called amplitude factors. Since it follows from the physical meaning of the problem that the critical value $q = q_0$ is attained comparatively rarely, the behavior of $q(t)$ must be investigated over a period of time which is long in comparison with the period of oscillation. For strictly harmonic oscillations the amplitudes $\alpha_i \sqrt{\varepsilon_i}$ and phases ψ_i are independent of time; however, to a first approximation the effect of slight anharmonicity will be to cause the amplitudes and the phases to become slowly changing functions of time. This effect will be unimportant for rapid processes, but the time behavior of the function $q(t)$ will be radically affected over the long times which are of interest for decomposition at low pressures.

For the considered model of strictly harmonic oscillations, Slater [130] analyzed the possible trajectories and evaluated the mean lifetime $\langle \tau \rangle$ on the basis of Eq. (4.1). Averaging over all possible trajectories implies first averaging with respect to the phases ψ_i of the normal coordinates and then, averaging with respect to the energies ε_i. The first averaging yields the frequency L with which the critical surface is intersected, which depends on the energy of the different normal coordinates. Finally, the averaging $1/L$ with respect to the energies of the normal coordinates under the condition of conservation of the total energy yields the mean lifetime $\langle \tau \rangle$. Slater did not derive the distribution function $h(\tau^*, E)$; generalization of the theory to the intermediate pressure range was based on the assumption of random distribution of the lifetimes. The corresponding expression for the rate constant at any pressure takes the form [cf. Eq. (2.9)]

$$\kappa = \int \frac{ZL\,(\varepsilon_1,\,\varepsilon_2,\,\ldots,\,\varepsilon_s)}{L(\varepsilon_1,\,\varepsilon_2,\,\ldots,\,\varepsilon_s)+Z}\exp\,(-\,\beta\Sigma\varepsilon_i)\prod_i d\,(\beta\varepsilon_i). \qquad (4.2)$$

In general, the function $L\,(\varepsilon_i)$ is quite complex and will not be reproduced here, but the nature of the function can be understood by considering the mean lifetime $\langle\tau\rangle$, which can be evaluated as follows. At low pressures Eq. (4.2) does not contain the function L and the integral can be evaluated quite simply [130]:

$$\kappa_0 = \tilde{v}\,(4\pi\beta E_0)^{\frac{s-1}{2}}\,\mu_1\mu_2\ldots\mu_s\exp\,(-\,\beta E_0), \qquad (4.3)$$

where μ_i are the normalized amplitude factors related to α_i by $\mu_i = \alpha_i/(\Sigma\alpha_i^2)^{1/2}$. It can also be shown that the frequency factor v determined from Eq. (3.4) is expressed in terms of the molecular frequency v_i and the coefficients μ_i by

$$\tilde{v} = [\sum_i \mu_i^2 v_i^2]^{1/2}. \qquad (4.4)$$

On the other hand, the quantity σ^*/F contained explicitly in Eq. (2.7) and implicitly in Eq. (4.2) is known, since it is exactly equal to the corresponding value in Kassel's theory: $\sigma^*/F = \tilde{v}\,(E - E_0)^{s-1}\beta^s$. Taking an inverse Laplace transform of Eq. (4.3) the following expression is obtained for $\langle\tau\rangle$:

$$\langle\tau\rangle = (\tilde{v})^{-1}\left(\frac{E - E_0}{4\pi E_0}\right)^{\frac{s-1}{2}}\cdot\frac{(s-1)!}{\left(\frac{s-1}{2}\right)!}\mu_1\ldots\mu_s. \qquad (4.5)$$

This expression is valid when $E - E_0 \ll E_0$ and when $\mu_i \gg ((E - E_0)/4\pi E_0)^{1/2}$. Any of the coefficients μ_j which are too small $(\mu_j < [(E - E_0)/4\pi E_0]^{1/2})$ must be omitted from Eq. (4.5) and the number of oscillators correspondingly reduced. Thus, it becomes clear that if in Slater's theory coupling of the reaction coordinate with some of the normal vibrations is very weak ($\mu^2_j < [(E-E_0)/4\pi E_0]^{1/2}$), the lifetime $\langle \tau \rangle$ will decrease.

It must finally be noted that the mean lifetime of an active molecule in Slater's theory [130] is less than that derived from Kassel's theory [6]. This will be easily understood if $\langle \tau \rangle$ is interpreted as the lifetime of the complex formed by bimolecular association of the reaction products. In the absence of anharmonicity the representative point passes through the region corresponding to the active molecule along a trajectory corresponding to purely harmonic motion. In the presence of slight anharmonicity (as in Kassel's theory) the representative point, in addition to moving along a trajectory, crosses slowly from trajectory to trajectory and, after a certain time, reaches a region of phase space from which it cannot possibly escape into the region of the reaction products along a trajectory of purely harmonic motion. If $1/L(\varepsilon_i)$ is averaged with respect to the energies of normal vibrations on the basis of an equiprobable distribution of ε_i, taking into account that region of phase space into which transition is possible only as a result of anharmonicity, the expression obtained for the mean lifetime will be identical with Eq. (3.5).

The s-fold integral of Eq. (4.2) can be reduced to a single integral, whereupon the expression obtained for the reduced reaction rate takes the form

$$\frac{\varkappa}{\varkappa_\infty} = \frac{1}{\left(\frac{s-1}{2}\right)!} \int\limits_0^\infty \frac{x^m \exp(-x)\,dx}{1+x^m\theta^{-1}}, \qquad (4.6)$$

where $\theta = (Z/\tilde{v})(4\pi\beta E_0)^m \mu_1...\mu_s$; $m = \frac{1}{2}(s-1)$ and the values of the coefficients μ_j are limited by the restrictions noted in the case of Eq. (4.5).

5. EFFECT OF ANHARMONICITY ON REACTION RATE

From a comparison of Eqs. (4.6) and (3.6) it is easy to see that by a suitable choice of the effective number of collisions Z, when $b \gg s$, the expressions for the reduced rate constant in the theories of Kassel and Slater coincide if the number of degrees of freedom of the activated molecule in Slater's theory is twice the number of degrees of freedom of the activated molecule in Kassel's theory.* The physical meaning of the difference between these theories is clear. The slight anharmonicity which is implicit in Kassel's theory significantly increases the phase-space hypervolume of the active molecule and simultaneously leads to a decrease in the difference in the effectiveness of the various degrees of freedom. In particular, this means that if Kassel's formula is used with an effective number of oscillators less than the true number of vibrational degrees of freedom to interpret experimental data, it is implicitly assumed that the interaction of the reaction coordinate with the noneffective degrees of freedom is less than the interaction between it and the other normal coordinates as a consequence of anharmonicity. This indicates the kinds of difficulties which arise in an attempt to separate the active and nonactive degrees of freedom.

At present only a few investigations of the effect of anharmonicity on the behavior of nuclei in a molecule have been reported. Thiele and Wilson [139], Bunker [52], Thiele [141], and Hung and Wilson [75] have described the use of computers for the investigation of the classical motion of nuclei in a model triatomic molecule with an anharmonic potential.

---

*The values of the parameters b and s for which this agreement occurs have been investigated by Schlag et al. [124].

The limits of applicability of a strictly harmonic model can be estimated approximately as follows. Anharmonicity affects mostly the exchange of energy between normal vibrations when the overtones (or fundamental) of one type of oscillation are close to the overtones of another type. In the case of exact resonance (for example, Fermi resonance in a triatomic molecule) the frequency of energy transfer can be equated to the change in the frequency of oscillation of the nucleus δv caused by the anharmonic terms of the potential. Since the anharmonicity constant in a polyatomic molecule is usually of the same order of magnitude as that in a diatomic molecule, δv can be evaluated, for example, on the basis of the Morse oscillator model. For a Morse oscillator the relationship between the frequency v and the vibrational energy E is of the form $v = v_0 \ [(E_0 - E)/E_0]^{1/2}$, where E_0 is the dissociation energy and v_0 is the frequency of small-amplitude oscillations. For a change in the frequency with respect to v_0

$$\delta v = v_0 - v \approx \frac{1}{2} v_0 \frac{E}{E_0}. \qquad (5.1)$$

The applicability of the harmonic model to a reacting molecule can be met only if the mean lifetime of the active molecule (calculated on the basis of the harmonic approximation) is appreciably shorter than the characteristic time τ_{anh} for energy transfer between normal oscillations, that is

$$\langle \tau \rangle \ll \tau_{anh}. \qquad (5.2)$$

If $1/\delta v$ from Eq. (5.1) is substituted for τ_{anh}, the condition of applicability of the harmonic model is obtained, since $1/\delta v$ gives the lower limit for τ_{anh}. It should be noted that the mean value of the energy of an active molecule per bond should be substituted for E in Eq. (5.1).

Unfortunately, since the above evaluation of τ_{anh} gives too strict a condition for the applicability of the harmonic model, the effect of anharmonicity on a vibrationally-excited molecule with an excitation energy of the order of the energy of a chemical bond must be investigated more thoroughly. This has been done by Thiele and Wilson [139] who studied a model of two dynamically coupled oscillators. They found that when the energy of symmetrical oscillations exceeded a certain value of $0.6\,E_0$, small antisymmetrical vibrations were unstable; their amplitude increases rapidly due to the transfer of energy from the symmetrical oscillations. Another model, investigated by Tredgold [142], in which the effect of anharmonicity on the exchange of energy between two oscillators of equal frequency could be followed analytically, also showed the importance of the effect of anharmonicity on intramolecular energy transfer.

The importance of the effect of anharmonicity revealed in calculations based on the above models does not, however, mean that there are no examples to which Slater's theory is applicable. Condition (5.2) can be fulfilled for nonadiabatic reactions in electronically excited states, when $\langle \tau \rangle$ can be small as a result of the relatively slight vibrational excitation.

The above considerations clearly indicate the need for a theory which takes into account the effect of anharmonicity on the dynamics of intramolecular motion. In the absence of such a theory, Slater's theory remains the only one which represents in detail the reaction mechanism.

The effect of anharmonicity on the rate of decomposition is reduced at high pressures, when the relative importance of the mechanism of intramolecular energy transfer becomes smaller. Therefore the frequency factor $\tilde{\nu}$, calculated within the framework of Slater's theory and characterizing the rate of unimolecular reactions at high pressures, changes only slightly as a result of anharmonicity [133]. The results of calculation of the frequency factor for the thermal isomerization of cyclopropane to propylene [67] are presented here (see table below) in order to show the dependence of the pre-exponential factor on the choice of the reaction coordinate q.

Variation of pre-exponential factor with choice
of reaction coordinate

Selected reaction coordinate	$\tilde{\nu} \cdot 10^{-14}$, sec^{-1}	Symmetry factor
Distance between chemically unconnected H. . .C atoms	4.5	12
Extension of the $C - C$ bond.	0.92	3
Difference between the distances H. . .C and $C - C$.	4.2	12
Total change in distance on extension of $C - C$ bond and opposite torsional oscillation of CH_2	1.68	3

6. ANOMALOUSLY HIGH PRE-EXPONENTIAL FACTORS FOR RATES OF THERMALLY-INDUCED UNIMOLECULAR REACTIONS

Within the limits of the oscillator models considered above, it is easy to see that the pre-exponential factor of the rate constant at high pressures is of the order of the frequency of molecular vibrations. Moreover, on the basis of small-perturbation theory it can be shown that the frequency $\tilde{\nu}$ in Eqs. (3.4) and (3.6) always lies between the lowest and highest frequencies of the active molecule and that the frequencies ν_i^* of the activated complex lie in an interval between the adjacent frequencies ν_i and ν_{i+1} of the active molecule. Nevertheless, the general thermodynamic treatment does not in principle set an upper limit to the value of the pre-exponential factor. Since, however, the pre-exponential factor

for the majority of unimolecular reactions which have been experimentally investigated is of the order of magnitude of the
frequency of vibration, those reactions for which the pre-
exponential factor exceeds 10^{14} sec^{-1} are frequently known as
reactions with anomalously high pre-exponential factors.

High pre-exponential factors are associated with the presence
of anharmonicity in the intramolecular vibrations. An estimate
of the anharmonicity can be made in a general form at high pressures when the lifetime of the active molecules does not determine the reaction rate.

To derive a general expression for the pre-exponential factor
at high pressures, Eyring's theory of the transition state can be
used [2]. Assume that in a small region, close to the intersection
of the trajectory of the representative point with the critical
surface, the variables in the Hamiltonian of the molecule are
approximately separable, so that the frequency of transition
through the critical surface along the reaction coordinate q for
the set of systems whose kinetic energies lie in the interval $d\varepsilon$ is

$$\frac{dN}{dt} = \left(\frac{v}{dq}\right)\frac{dp\,dq}{2\pi\hbar} = \frac{d\varepsilon}{2\pi\hbar}. \tag{6.1}$$

Averaging over the remaining degrees of freedom can be carried
out using the equilibrium distribution function $\exp\left[-\beta H(p_i, q_i)\right]$ in
which the reaction coordinate is fixed, that is, $q = q_0$. This distribution function must obviously be normalized to a unit concentration of the reactant molecules which, for a given number of
particles, is proportional to the sum of states of the molecules.
Thus the following expression is obtained for the rate constant of
unimolecular reaction:

$$\kappa_\infty = \frac{F^*}{F}\exp\left(-\beta E_0\right)\int_0^\infty \exp\left(-\beta\varepsilon\right)\frac{d\varepsilon}{2\pi\hbar} = \frac{kT}{2\pi\hbar}\cdot\frac{F^*}{F}\exp\left(-\beta E_0\right), \tag{6.2}$$

where F^* is the total partition function of the activated complex. It will easily be seen that the application of this expression to the oscillator model leads to formula (3.6) for κ_∞. In fact, for this model the effect of the contribution of only the vibrational partition functions should be taken into account, each of which for the ith normal vibration of the molecule is equal to $kT/\hbar\omega_i$ (or $kT/\hbar\omega_i^*$ for the activated complex). Thus, without a correction for strong anharmonicity the oscillator model cannot explain the high values of the pre-exponential factors.

The reaction rate for a model with strong anharmonicity can also be derived on the basis of Eq. (6.2). In calculating the partition function of the reactant molecules the effect of anharmonicity can be neglected in the majority of cases. Consider, for example, the calculation of the partition function of an activated molecule similar to ethane, assuming that the reaction coordinate is the extension of a $C - C$ bond, which leads to dissociation. It is natural to assume that on extension of the $C - C$ bond the force constant of torsional vibration will decrease, so that in the critical configuration $(q = q_0)$ the torsional vibration can be transformed into free rotation. In this case it is obvious that the calculated partition function corresponding to torsional vibration in the activated molecule must be replaced by the partition function of a one-dimensional rotator. The "normal" value of the pre-exponential factor will then be multiplied by

$$\frac{F_{\text{rot}}}{F_{\text{vib}}} \approx \frac{(2\pi I k T)^{1/2}v}{kT}, \tag{6.3}$$

which at low temperatures is significantly greater than unity.

Steel and Laidler [135, 136] and Slater [132] have investigated the relationship between the statistical sums of activated complexes and the reaction coordinates.

Formula (6.2) for the reaction rate constant is precise if F^* denotes the total partition function of the activated molecule. The difficulty then reduces to the accurate determination of the critical surface. This problem is generally extremely complex. On the one hand, interaction of the reaction coordinate close to the critical surface with the remaining internal degrees of freedom must be weak, since this surface separates the reactant molecules from the reaction products. On the other hand, interaction of the reaction coordinate with degrees of freedom which are not participating directly in the reaction must be strong enough to provide a high rate of activation. In fact, qualitatively speaking, unimolecular reactions can be represented as proceeding in two stages: thermal activation by collisions and spontaneous decomposition as the result of random redistribution of energy. The rate of the process is determined by the rate of the slowest stage, which is the reason for the pressure dependence of the decomposition rate. It follows that the constant κ_∞ as given by Eq. (6.2) must also be less than the activation rate constant κ_{act}, which, for example, for a statistical model of a system of classical oscillators is given by $\kappa_{act} = Z[(\beta E_0)^{s-1}/(s-1)!] \exp(-\beta E_0)$. From physical considerations it is clear that the weaker the interaction of the reaction coordinate with the remaining degrees of freedom, the smaller the effective number of the degrees of freedom which contribute to the activation rate. Thus, finally, the necessary inequality $\kappa_{act} \gg \kappa_\infty$ will cease to exist. The coupling of the reaction coordinate with the other degrees of freedom can cause the representative point to describe a very complex trajectory close to the critical surface. This means that if the critical surface is not determined exactly, the representative point may enter the region of the reaction products and then return to the region of the reactants, and so on. Therefore, for all cases in which the critical surface is determined on the basis of simple qualitative considerations, a multiplier χ must be introduced into Eq. (6.2) to take into account the "reflection" of the representative point (χ is known as the transmission coefficient). The evaluation of χ presents an extremely difficult problem which is complicated by the fact that, in principle, the reaction coordinate cannot be the "normal" coordinate of the Hamiltonian of the molecule. To clarify this consider Slater's model, for which the thermal decomposition rate at high pressures is given by Eq. (3.6). This expression is valid only if the rate of activation

$$\kappa_{\text{act}} = Z \left(4\pi\beta E_0\right)^{\frac{s-1}{2}} \mu_1 \ldots \mu_s \exp\left(-\beta E_0\right) \tag{6.4}$$

is greater than the rate of spontaneous decomposition (3.6). If the reaction coordinate q is normal, all the coefficients μ_i except one must be equal to zero and consequently must, by the rule given for the evaluation of Eq. (4.6), be omitted from Eq. (4.3), simultaneously setting $s = 1$. It is easy to see that the necessary condition $\kappa_{\text{act}} \gg \kappa_\infty$, which can here be expressed in the form $Z \gg \tilde{v}$ will never be fulfilled under the conditions of gas kinetics.

Calculation of the rate of unimolecular decomposition for a series of complex molecules and ions by Ree, Eyring, and Fueno [111] shows that in many cases it is necessary to assume free three-dimensional rotation of radicals in the activated molecule, which in the stable molecule corresponds to torsional and deformational vibration. Only in this case is it possible to explain the high values of the pre-exponential factor (as high as 10^{17}-10^{18} sec^{-1}). The transmission coefficient apparently ranges from 1 to 0.1 for various adiabatic dissociation reactions [111].

Finally, it should be noted that the general expression (6.2) can also be used for calculating the reaction rates for cases in which two or more bonds are ruptured simultaneously. In this case, of course, several reaction coordinates are involved, but the general method of calculation remains the same as in the case of a single reaction coordinate [131, 138].

Chapter II

THE QUANTUM THEORY OF UNIMOLECULAR
REACTIONS

Quantum theories of unimolecular reactions are based, in principle, on the same concepts as classical theories, but intra- and intermolecular energy exchange must be described by a non-stationary matrix of densities of the energy levels of the molecule and not by a set of classical trajectories in phase space. It is necessary to develop a quantum theory of unimolecular reactions because, for the majority of polyatomic molecules, reaction occurs at a temperature which is not high in comparison with the characteristic vibrational temperature $\hbar\omega/k$. Moreover, investigation of the problem of intermolecular energy exchange has shown that quantization of intramolecular motion must be taken into account. Theory and the existing experimental data show that the probability of converting translational into vibrational energy is low if the lower vibrational levels are involved. As the vibrational quantum number increases, the probability of such conversion is increased as a result of the greater amplitude of the vibrations and the decrease in size of the vibrational quanta. These effects occur for all molecules, including diatomic molecules, for which there is a more or less complete theory of translational-vibrational energy exchange for the lower vibrational levels (e.g., see [7]). In the case of polyatomic molecules, anharmonicity of the vibrations, which leads to interaction between the normal coordinates, also plays an important part. In spite of the relatively large size of vibrational quanta, the spectrum of a vibrationally-excited complex molecule is almost continuous as a result of the large number of degrees of freedom. If it is taken into consideration that the probability of vibrational-translational energy exchange depends principally on the amount of energy to be transferred and that this in turn depends, for a complex molecule, less on the size of the vibrational quanta than on the intensity of the interaction between the normal coordinates, the important role of anharmonicity in the process of intermolecular energy exchange will become clear. At present it is impossible to achieve a convincing calculation of the cross sections of inelastic activating collisions for vibrationally excited polyatomic molecules. Therefore it is of interest to investigate various models which correspond qualitatively to various mechanisms of inter- and intramolecular energy exchange. By comparing the results obtained with experimental data it will be possible to see how successfully a given model represents the true reaction mechanism.

7. KASSEL'S MODEL

The mechanism of strong activating collisions. The quantum-mechanical variant of Kassel's theory [6] is, like the classical theory, based on the assumption of the statistical redistribution of energy in a system of s identical oscillators which represents the molecule. Therefore, Eqs. (1.1) or (1.3) can be used in calculating the probability of formation of the activated state, which

in this case is defined only in the quasi-classical approximation
(see Section 1). Here the entropy S or the statistical weight $g(n)$
must be employed to take into account the quantization of the
levels. Since the model consists of identical oscillators its spectrum is a series of equidistant levels separated by a distance $\hbar\omega$,
the degeneracy of the level of energy E_n being $g_s(n)$, which is
given by

$$g_s(n) = (n + s - 1)! / (s - 1)! \, n! \qquad (7.1)$$

It is clear that this model is very far from reality, since the
vibrational levels for a real polyatomic molecule give, as was
noted above, an almost continuous spectrum. If the critical energy E_0 corresponds to a vibrational level $n_0 = E_0/\hbar\omega$, the probability of formation of the activated state will, in accordance
with Eq. (1.1), be given by

$$W = g_s(n - n_0) / g_s(n) \qquad (7.2)$$

and the rate of decomposition will be obtained by multiplying this
probability by the frequency factor $\tilde{v}$. From the meaning of the
problem it will be clear that in the case of dissociation $\tilde{v}$ must be
of the order of the frequency of oscillations of the nuclei, 10^{13}-
10^{14} sec^{-1}, as in the classical treatment. It should now be noted
that within the limits of the statistical model under discussion it
can be assumed that the reaction times are randomly distributed
with a distribution function of the type given by Eq. (2.8). For the
processes of intermolecular energy exchange and spontaneous
dissociation a kinetic equation can then be written, describing
transitions between stationary levels caused by either collisions
or dissociation (see Section 2). If x_i denotes the population of the
ith level, and P_{ij} is the dimensionless probability of transition
from the ith level to the jth level, the balance equations will take

the form

$$\frac{dx_i}{dt} = \sum_j Z_0 P_{ji} x_j - \sum_j Z_0 P_{ij} x_i - \tilde{v} g_s (i - n_0) / g_s (i) \qquad (7.3)$$

(it will be assumed hereafter that when $i < n_0$, $g(i - n_0)$ is equal to zero). Here Z_0 denotes the number of gas-kinetic collisions per unit time between the reactant molecules AB and the molecules of the gas M which lead to the activation of AB. The probabilities of the forward and reverse processes, P_{ij} and P_{ji}, are related by the principle of detailed balancing

$$P_{ij} g_s (i) \exp (- \beta E_i) = P_{ji} g_s (j) \exp (- \beta E_j). \qquad (7.4)$$

In Kassel's theory, which is usually considered as the simplest theory of unimolecular reaction, it is assumed that the rate of activation, which is given by the first term in Eq. (7.3), is always equal to the rate of activation under equilibrium conditions (the assumption of strong activating collisions*), that is, that

$$\sum_j Z_0 P_{jk} x_j = Z x_k^0, \qquad (7.5)$$

where $x_k^0 = g_s(\kappa) \exp (-\beta \hbar \omega \kappa)/F(s)$, Z is the effective number of collisions per unit time, and $F(s) = [1 - \exp (-\beta \hbar \omega)]^s$.

The condition that a Boltzmann distribution is established in the absence of reaction means that, in general,

$$\sum_j Z_0 P_{\kappa j} x_\kappa = Z x_\kappa. \qquad (7.6)$$

Thus an equation of the form

$$\frac{dx_i}{dt} = - Z (x_i - x_i^0) - \kappa_i x_i; \quad \kappa_i = \kappa (E_i) = \tilde{v} g_s (i - n_0) / g_s (i), \qquad (7.7)$$

is obtained, which can easily be solved in the quasi-classical approximation. Assuming that $dx_i / dt = 0$,

---

*Ed. Note: For a complete discussion of strong activation cf. p. 6.

$$x_i = Z x_i^0 / (Z + \kappa_i). \tag{7.8}$$

The reaction rate constant κ can obviously be expressed in the form

$$\kappa = \sum_i \kappa_i x_i = \sum_i \frac{Z \kappa_i x_i^0}{Z + \kappa_i}. \tag{7.9}$$

This formula is the quantum analog of Eq. (2.3). The limiting value of the rate constant at high pressures is

$$\kappa_\infty = \tilde{\nu} \exp(-\beta E_0). \tag{7.10}$$

At low pressures

$$\kappa_0 = Z g_s (n_0) \exp(-\beta \hbar \omega n_0) / F (s - 1). \tag{7.11}*$$

For intermediate pressures the rate constant can be conveniently expressed in the form

$$\frac{\kappa}{\kappa_\infty} = (1 - e^{-\theta})^s \sum_{n=0}^{\infty} \frac{g_s (n) \exp(-n\theta)}{1 + \tilde{\nu} g_s (n) / Z g_s (n + n_0)}, \tag{7.12}$$

where $\theta = \beta \hbar \omega$. This equation is the quantum analog of Eq. (3.8).

The following comments should be noted in connection with Eqs. (7.11) and (3.7). In evaluating the integrals in Eqs. (2.6) and (2.7) it is usually assumed that $s \ll \beta E_0$. This means that on summing over all the excited states which affect the reaction rate and which, in accordance with the conclusions of statistical theory (see Section 1), have energies close to the critical energy E_0, the distribution function of the system of s oscillators is assumed to be approximately exponential. The relative error introduced into Eq. (3.7) by this assumption is of the order of $s/\beta E_0$. At lower temperatures this error decreases and, for Kassel's model, when $\theta > 1$ it becomes $\exp(-\theta) \hbar \omega / E_0$. However, it must be noted that

*Cf. Editor's Note following Eq. (7.13).

for the more realistic models of a molecule with various frequencies, the statistical weight $g_s(E_0)$ is usually not evaluated precisely but on the basis of some approximation. For example, for the semi-classical approximation [see Eq. (9.11) below] the relative error in the evaluation of $g_s(E_0)$ is of the order of

$$[\Gamma(s)\langle v_i^2\rangle / 6s\Gamma(s-2)\langle v_i\rangle^2]\,[E_z/(E_0+E_z)]^2, \qquad (7.13)$$

where E_z is the total energy of the zero-point vibrations of the molecule [68]. In the majority of cases of practical interest the error due to the imprecise evaluation of $g_s(E_0)$ exceeds the error which is introduced by neglecting the energy-dependence of the statistical weight for energies close to E_0 in comparison with the Boltzmann multiplier.*

Stepwise activation. Nonequilibrium distribution function. Since it is at present difficult to produce definite concepts, even of a qualitative nature, about the rate of activation, it will be of interest to investigate the case of stepwise excitation as an alternative to the above mechanism of strong collisions, the latter case being one in which the rate of activation is always the equilibrium rate. For this case Buff and Wilson [48] suggested that molecular collisions cause transitions only between adjacent vibrational levels of the oscillators which represent the molecule. If it is assumed that the intermolecular interaction which produces an inelastic transition is proportional to the amplitudes of the vibrations of the oscillators, then, to the first approximation of perturbation theory, the interaction will change the quantum number of a single oscillator by unity and the probability of transition from level n to level $n+1$ will be proportional to $n+1$,

---

*Ed. Note: This follows from the Taylor expansion of $g_s(n)$ around n_0,

$$k_0 = \frac{Ze^{-\beta E_0}}{F(s)}\left[\frac{g_s(n_0)}{(1-e^{-\theta})} + \frac{g_s'(n_0)e^{-\theta}}{(1-e^{-\theta})^2} + \cdots\right].$$

i.e., $P_{n,\,n+1} = P_{0,1}\,(n+1)$. If the transition probability is averaged over all the states of the degenerate level E_n of the system of s identical oscillators, an expression is obtained for the probability of transition from level n to level $n+1$ which takes the form

$$P_{n,n+1} = P_{1,0}\exp\,(-\,\theta)\times(n+s), \qquad (7.14)$$

where $P_{1,0}$ is a constant which depends on the nature of the intermolecular interaction and is equal to the probability of deactivation of the first vibrational quantum. A system of kinetic equations obtained for the transition probability in Eq. (7.14) has been considered in [48]. The solution of these equations by a method analogous to the method of quasi-stationary concentrations leads to the following limiting values for the decomposition rate constant at high and low pressures (if $n_0 \gg s$):

$$\kappa_\infty = \tilde{v}\exp\,(-\,\beta n_0\hbar\omega), \qquad (7.15)$$

$$\kappa_0 = ZP_{1,0}\,(1-e^{-\theta})\,n_0 g_s\,(n_0)\exp\,(-\,\beta n_0\hbar\omega)\,/\,F\,(s-1). \qquad (7.16)$$

Comparison of the two mechanisms of activation is only possible if the rate constants are expressed in a dimensionless form, since neither the coefficient Z nor the probability $P_{1,0}$ can be evaluated with the necessary accuracy.

The expression for the rate constant at any pressure for the mechanism of stepwise excitation has in general a relatively complex form [48] and will not be cited here. Figure 1 shows the relationship between κ/κ_∞ and $\kappa_0 M/\kappa_\infty$ (the multiplier M is equal to the concentration of the molecules of the inert gas M). The continuous curves represent the relationship in the case of stepwise excitation for $s = 8$ and $s = 9$, and the dashed curve represents the case of strong collisions for $s = 10$. The curves are very close together, and thus it is unlikely that the interpretation of experimental data using semi-empirical values of the parameters s and Z could distinguish the mechanisms.

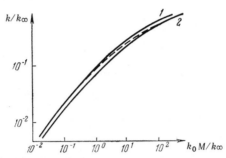

FIG. 1. Relationship between rate constant of unimolecular decomposition and pressure for a stepwise excitation mechanism (curve 1, $s = 8$; curve 2, $s = 9$) and a strong collision mechanism (dashed curve, $s = 10$); $\exp(-\theta) = 0.6$.

However, Hung and Wilson [74] have shown that the two mechanisms can be differentiated by investigating a unimolecular decomposition which can proceed by a reaction scheme that allows two different paths simultaneously:

$$
\begin{aligned}
AB \xrightarrow{\varkappa_1} A_1 + B_1, && E_0^{(1)} = n_0^{(1)} \hbar\omega, \\
AB \xrightarrow{\varkappa_2} A_2 + B_2, && E_0^{(2)} = n_0^{(2)} \hbar\omega, \\
n_0^{(1)} < n_0^{(2)}. &&
\end{aligned}
\tag{7.17}
$$

In this case the ratio of the rate constants $\varkappa_1/\varkappa_2$ at low pressures differs significantly for the two mechanisms. The results of a calculation for a model system are shown in Fig. 2. The increase in the ratio $\varkappa_1/\varkappa_2$ on decreasing the pressure of the gas M can be interpreted as follows. The reaction with the lower energy of activation causes depletion of the levels which lie above $E_0^{(1)}$; as a result the rate of the second reaction is less than would be expected in the absence of the first reaction. Obviously the more

k_1/k_2

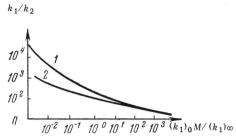

FIG. 2. Relationship between the ratio of rate constants of two parallel unimolecular decomposition reactions and pressure. Curve 1—stepwise activation mechanism, $s = 15$; curve 2—strong collision mechanism, $s = 17$. Parameters of the model are: $\exp(-\theta) = 0.6$; $n_0^{(2)} - n_0^{(1)} = 5$; $\widetilde{v_2}/\widetilde{v_1} = 1.13$.

localized the distribution function of the transferred energy is, the more the equilibrium distribution above the lower reaction threshold will be disturbed. A calculation of the nonequilibrium distribution function by Nikitin [18] for an analogous model under the condition $\theta \ll 1$ shows that above the threshold of the first reaction this function can be expressed in the form

$$x(E) \approx \exp\left\{-\frac{f(E)}{2} - \int_{E_0}^{E} \left[\left(\frac{f'}{2}\right)^2 + \frac{\kappa(E)}{D}\right]^{1/2} d(\beta E)\right\}. \qquad (7.18)$$

The pre-exponential terms which are not important for a general discussion have been omitted here and the symbol $f(E) = \beta E - s\ln(\beta E) + \ln s!$ has been introduced; D represents the ratio of mean square energy transferred per unit time to $(kT)^2$. The equilibrium distribution function is obtained from Eq. (7.18) when $D \gg \kappa(E)$.

For the mechanism of strong collisions, for which Eqs. (7.7) and (7.8) are valid

$$x(E) = \exp[-f(E)]\frac{Z}{Z + \kappa(E)}. \qquad (7.19)$$

If the parameters Z and D in the above two expressions are selected so that the rate constants in the limiting cases of high and low pressure coincide, it follows that $Z = D$. Hence, it becomes evident that the nonequilibrium population of a level $x(E)$ depends on the nature of the activation process.

The thermal decomposition of ethyl bromide (investigated by Shilov [33]) is apparently an example of a decomposition which can proceed by two distinct paths. In this case the primary reactions are

$$C_2H_5Br \rightarrow HBr + C_2H_4 \quad E_0^{(1)} = 53 \text{ kcal/mole,}$$
$$(7.20)$$
$$C_2H_5Br \rightarrow \dot{B}r + \dot{C}_2H_5 \quad E_0^{(2)} = 65 \text{ kcal/mole.}$$

The second of these reactions can lead to a chain process of decomposition:

$$\dot{B}r + C_2H_5Br \rightarrow \dot{C}_2H_4Br + HBr,$$
$$(7.21)$$
$$\dot{C}_2H_4Br \rightarrow C_2H_4 + \dot{B}r.$$

It was found that in this case, when in accordance with the general behavior of chain reactions process (7.21) should have caused an increase in the rate of decomposition, such an increase did not occur. However, addition of $\dot{B}r$ atoms did increase the rate of decomposition. Investigations of the pressure dependence of the relative yield of reactions of the type (7.17) should in principle lead to the understanding of the mechanism of vibrational activation.

Since the rate of activation must depend on the properties of the molecules of M, information about the process of activation should be obtainable from investigations of the effect of various gases on the rate of unimolecular reaction. Unfortunately, it is difficult to conduct such a study at the present time, since there are no theoretical methods for calculation of the probability of energy transfer for molecules under high vibrational excitation. However, on the basis of extremely general theoretical principles it can be shown that for a series of cases the relationship between the probability of transition P and the energy change ΔE is of the form

$$P \approx \exp\left[-\left|\Delta E\right| a / \hbar v^{*}\right], \qquad (7.22)$$

where a is the characteristic radius of interaction and v^{*} is the relative velocity of those colliding molecules which make the greatest contribution to the probability of the inelastic transition. For large values of ΔE, when the exponent is appreciably greater than unity, v^{*} is itself a function of ΔE. In this case an expression is obtained which is known as the Landau-Teller formula [7, 87]

$$P \approx \exp\left\{- \text{const}\left[\mu\left(\Delta E\right)^{2} / T\right]^{1/3}\right\}. \qquad (7.23)$$

Using Eqs. (7.22) and (7.23) to relate the rate of activation to the reduced mass of the colliding molecules μ and the nature of intermolecular interaction, it is possible to determine the value of ΔE, which qualitatively characterizes the amount of energy transferred. Such a calculation has been carried out by Mahan [92] for the decomposition of NO_2Cl in the presence of various inert gases. Using values of a which are normally assumed in calculations of vibrational relaxation times, Mahan found that $\Delta E \approx 12$ cm^{-1}. This result apparently shows that, for the investigated reaction, activation proceeds by the successive transfer of small amounts of energy. However, it must be remembered that a relationship such as (7.22) is only obtained for molecular transitions $i \rightarrow j$ for which the initial i and final j states are characterized by an almost identical intermolecular interaction. In this case the relative spacing of the vibrational terms of the system of two colliding molecules will be little affected by the intermolecular distance, and transition from the initial to the final state can be represented as transition between the potential curves i and j shown in Fig. 3 (continuous curves). The exponential relationship between the probability of transition and the energy transferred is due to the fact that the potential curves for i and j are characterized by a constant energy difference ΔE. If as the result of intramolecular interaction the curves were to approach one another or intersect, the probability of transition would be greatly increased. For diatomic molecules the only such inter-action which is possible is a nonadiabatic electronic-vibrational interaction, which does in fact cause a large increase in the probability of transition [19, 99]. For a polyatomic molecule, however, another possibility exists. It can happen that, as the

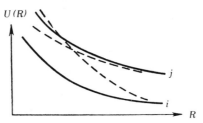

FIG. 3. Possible types of potential curves for the interaction between AB and M, corresponding to different vibrational states of AB. R is the distance between AB and M.

result of anharmonic interactions, initial and final states of a polyatomic molecule which do not differ greatly in their energy are characterized by an appreciable difference in the amplitudes of oscillation of some atom or group of atoms. In this case the energies of interaction of these states can differ appreciably and the i and j curves may intersect (Fig. 3, dashed curves). It is possible that such transitions are responsible for the large amount of energy loss per collision that has been observed in investigations involving the deactivation of vibrationally highly-excited complex molecules subsequent to chemical activation or photoexcitation [83]. It is probable that the frequently proposed hypothesis of the formation of a short-lived complex of the colliding molecules, within which statistical redistribution of energy can occur [83], is valid within the limits of the above concepts. It is obviously necessary in this case to take into account the intersection of the initial terms i with many of the final terms j.

It might also be expected that the mechanism of activating collisions could be deduced from investigations of the pressure dependence of the fluorescence spectrum of molecules participating in photochemical decomposition reactions. Such processes are characterized by a quantum yield for the reaction and an intensity for the individual vibrational bands. The calculations of Porter and Connelly [103] and Wilson et al. [153] showed that the quantum yield is scarcely affected by the details of inelastic molecular collisions and that it is thus apparently impossible to draw any definite conclusions about the possible mechanisms of activation.* However, the distribution of intensity in the spectrum does depend on the mechanism—single-quantum or multiple-quantum—of vibrational deactivation of the electronically excited states of the radiating molecule. Although it is difficult to establish the necessary experimental conditions, Levitt [88] was able to observe the depopulation, caused by the predissociation $NO_2^* \rightarrow NO + O$, of the vibrational levels in an emission spectrum from NO_2^* excited by molecular collisions behind a shock front. Levitt found that the relative disturbance of the equilibrium distribution

---

*Ed. Note: Recent evidence indicates that under certain extreme conditions of pressure and energy such information is obtainable, at least crudely.

below the predissociation limit is of the form

$$x(E) / x^0(E) \approx \left(1 - \exp\frac{E - E_0}{kT}\right), \qquad (7.24)$$

where E is the energy of the vibrational level and E_0 is the dissociation limit [88]. The same relationship is obtained by a theoretical calculation of the nonequilibrium distribution function in dissociation reactions for a stepwise activation mechanism [14, 97, 98].

Strong and weak coupling between normal vibrations. The assumption in Kassel's theory of a statistical redistribution of vibrational energy implies, in fact, the existence of strong anharmonic interaction between the oscillators which does not, however, appreciably affect the vibrational spectrum. Any detailed theory of intramolecular energy transfer must explicitly take into account the effect of anharmonicity. This can be done by assuming that there is a characteristic mean time for the random exchange of quanta between the oscillators of the molecule. The probability that n quanta will be concentrated on a single (active) oscillator which represents the dissociating bond will then be given, not by Eq. (7.2), but by the solution of a kinetic equation which describes the intramolecular redistribution of energy and the spontaneous decomposition (or isomerization) of the molecule. In this case the fraction of molecules which are active $P^{(n)}$ will be a complex function of time. By analogy with Eq. (2.3)

$$\varkappa = Z \sum_{n=n_0}^{\infty} x_n^0 \int_0^{\infty} \left(-\frac{dP^{(n)}}{dt}\right) \exp(-Zt)\, dt, \qquad (7.25)$$

where the integral within the summation sign gives the probability of spontaneous decomposition averaged over the distribution of lifetimes of the active molecule, and summation over n gives the rate of equilibrium activation.

Wilson [152] and Brauner and Wilson [45] have investigated a simple model of intramolecular energy transfer by assuming that the interaction of the active oscillator with the remaining oscillators of the molecule is proportional to its vibrational energy. In this case the proportion of active molecules $P_m^{(n)}$, for which the total energy is $E_n = \hbar \omega n$, of which $E_m = \hbar \omega m$ is concentrated in the active oscillator, is given by the following kinetic equations [45]:

$$\frac{dP_m^{(n)}}{dt} = \gamma m \, (n - m - 1) \, P_{m-1}^{(n)} + \gamma \, (m + 1) \, (n + s - m - 2) \, P_{m+1}^{(n)} - \\ - \gamma \, [(m + 1) \, (n - m) + m \, (n + s - m - 1)] \, P_m^{(n)} - \tilde{v} U \, (m - n_0) \, P_m^{(n)}. \tag{7.26}$$

The first three terms on the right-hand side of this system of n equations describe transitions between adjacent levels in the active molecule, $m \to m \pm 1$, due to interaction with other oscillators of the molecule; the parameter γ characterizes the rate of such transitions. The final term represents spontaneous decomposition which occurs from all levels $m \geqslant n_0$ of an active oscillator of frequency $\tilde{v}$; the function $U(m - n_0)$ is equal to unity when $m \geqslant n_0$ and is equal to 0 when $m < n_0$. In the limiting case n, $s \to \infty$, $\tilde{v}/\gamma \ll 1$, $n\gamma = $ constant, the system (7.26) becomes a system of equations similar to (20.1) describing the relaxation and dissociation of a "cut-off" quantum oscillator in a heat bath. This is quite natural, since a complex molecule can be considered under some circumstances as a heat bath with respect to the degrees of freedom characterizing a particular chemical reaction. Expression (7.26) differs from (20.1) in that it takes into account the fact that excitation of the active oscillator causes "cooling" of the heat bath (it is indeed this circumstance this is responsible for the quadratic dependence of the probability of the transitions $m \to m \pm 1$ on m, which disappears when $n \gg m$). The function $P^{(n)}$ in Eq. (7.25) is obtained from $P_m^{(n)}$ by averaging over the various initial distributions of the active oscillator after collision of the reactant molecule with the inert molecule M. The function $P^{(n)}(t)$ can be described for the general case as a sum of terms which decreases exponentially with time. Therefore, the expression for κ obtained by integration of Eq. (7.25) is analogous to Eq. (7.9) if the partial rate constants κ_i are assumed to be functions of Z. This assumption implies, however, that the rates κ_i cannot be interpreted as the rate constants of spontaneous decomposition. This in turn shows that Lindeman's approach is not applicable to such a model. Only in the limiting case of very rapid intramolecular redistribution of energy, when $\gamma \gg \tilde{\nu}$, are expressions (7.7) and (7.9) obtained for κ_i and κ, respectively. Here, however, violation of the initial assumption of the small effect of anharmonicity on the structure of the vibrational spectrum of the molecule is possible. At present it is not clear which model of the kinetics of the statistical redistribution of energy is described by the system of equations (7.26). It should be noted, however, that Eq. (7.26) corresponds to the case (which in a certain sense is the opposite of Slater's quantum model) in which the redistribution of energy occurs as the result of dynamic beats in a system of oscillators.

For the model under consideration, Brauner and Wilson [45] found that the dimensionless rate constant κ/κ_∞ in the intermediate pressure range was less than the rate constant derived from Kassel's model and that the decrease in the rate of intramolecular energy transfer caused a widening of the transitional region of the pressure fall-off.

8. SLATER'S MODEL

The agreement between the high pressure rate constants κ_∞ for decomposition or isomerization derived for Kassel's and Slater's models in the classical approximation is connected with the fact that the rate of reaction for either of these models can be determined as the mean rate of intersection of the critical surface by the representative point [with the reaction rate calculated from the equilibrium distribution $P(q_0)$]. For a critical surface of the form $q = q_0$ it is obviously possible to express κ_∞ in the form

$$\kappa_\infty = \langle \dot{q} \rangle \, P \, (q_0). \tag{8.1}$$

In generalizing Eq. (8.1) to the quantum case it should above all be noted that the reaction condition, which is formulated as the condition for intersection of the critical surface $q = q_0$, is not as clearly defined for the quantum model as for the classical model. This situation exists because there is no correspondence between the reaction coordinate q_0 and the threshold energy E_0 in the quantum model, because chemical reactions can, in general, proceed by a tunneling process. It follows that the quantum theory of chemical reaction should be based on an evaluation of the contribution of the tunnel effect to the rate constant. Although this problem has been considered recently in a general form by several investigators [3, 4, 41], it is nevertheless difficult to make any concrete evaluation of the tunnel effect in various reactions, since the potential energy surface must be known. The indeterminacy of the relationship between q_0 and E_0 can be removed by assuming, for example, that the tunnel effect is insignificant at levels for which $E < E_0$. Such an assumption is made in Kassel's quantum model and in the quasi-equilibrium theory of chemical reactions. On the other hand, it may be assumed that the condition of intersection of the surface $q = q_0$ (including the "tunnel-effect" intersections) and relationship (8.1) are valid at any energy.* Here, of course, the question of the relationship between the implicit allowance for the tunnel effect in (8.1) and the proper correction for tunneling which must be made in the case of real potential energy surfaces, remains open.

Slater [130] bases the quantum-mechanical generalization of his theory on Eq. (8.1) and replaces the classical distribution function of the coordinate q and velocity $\dot{q}$, which is used in the derivation of Eq. (3.6), by the Wigner quantum-mechanical distribution function $W(\dot{q}, q)$. This function is obtained by a Fourier transform of the equilibrium density matrix of the system of harmonic oscillators. Corresponding calculations show [130] that the distribution over the velocities and coordinates is Gaussian (as in the classical case) with the mean square deviations σ^2 and $\dot{\sigma}^2$ for the coordinate q and the velocity $\dot{q}$ given by

$$\sigma^2 = \frac{1}{2} kT \sum_i \alpha_i^2 \frac{\theta_i}{2} \cot \frac{\theta_i}{2},$$

$$\dot{\sigma}^2 = \frac{1}{2} kT \sum_i \alpha_i^2 \omega_i^2 \frac{\theta_i}{2} \cot \frac{\theta_i}{2}, \qquad (8.2)$$

$$\theta_i = \hbar \omega_i / kT.$$

After averaging of Eq. (8.1) the following result is obtained [130]:

$$\kappa_\infty = \dot{\sigma} \, (2\pi\sigma)^{-1} \exp\left(- q_0^2 / 2\sigma^2\right). \qquad (8.3)$$

---

*An analogous approach to the calculation of the rate of unimolecular reactions has been reported by Mayants [11].

The principal difference between this formula and Eq. (3.6) is that the temperature dependence of the rate constant in Eq. (8.3) is not of the Arrhenius type when $\theta_i \gtrsim 1$. This is due to the very large contribution of tunneling transitions to the rate constant κ_∞. It has been shown [100] that tunneling transitions can have such a large effect only in the case of a resonance transition through a potential barrier separating two identical wells (for example, in the inversion of ammonia). For transitions of this type the rate constant κ_∞ is equal to the splitting of the levels of the double potential well, averaged over all the energy levels [91]. On the other hand, this splitting is related to the probability of finding the system at the center of the potential barrier as well as to the tunneling rate at this point as given by equations of the type (8.1) [100].

It must be understood that the harmonic approximation is obviously unsuitable for the description of tunneling rates, since this assumes the existence of a potential barrier of a shape approximated by two intersecting parabolas. However, as the result of the exponential dependence of κ_∞ on the critical value of the reaction coordinate q_0, the inverse relationship of determining q_0 is little affected by changes in the value of κ_∞. Consequently, the interpretation of experimental data on the basis of Eq. (8.3) is bound to yield reasonable values for q_0. Thus, for example, in the *cis-trans* isomerization of substituted ethylenes the critical configuration corresponds to a rotation of $\pi/2$ about the double bond. However, if such a value were in fact derived from the experimental value of κ_∞, it would not necessarily indicate the accuracy of the harmonic model.

Slater has shown [130] that if Eq. (8.3) is expressed formally as an Arrhenius equation with an experimental activation energy

$$E_{\mathrm{act}} = kT^2 \frac{d}{dT} \ln \kappa_\infty,$$

the effective pre-exponential factor must be appreciably less than the normal value of 10^{13}-10^{14} $\sec^{-1}$. This conclusion is particularly interesting because a series of isomerization reactions are in fact characterized by small frequency factors, which is usually interpreted as the result of nonadiabatic transition through an intermediate triplet state [2].

The probability of tunneling transitions in a dissociation process, when the molecule changes from a quasi-stationary state of the discrete spectrum to states with a continuous energy spectrum (such as a predissociation process by tunneling), is significantly less than the probability of resonance transitions between discrete levels [100]. Therefore, in investigating decomposition reactions it would seem to be more reasonable to completely neglect the effect of tunneling processes rather than to allow for the effect in accordance with Eq. (8.3). The harmonic model in the quantized form will then lead to an expression for the rate constant at high pressure κ_∞ of the same type as in the case of slight anharmonicity [Eq. (7.10)].

In extending the model to intermediate and low pressures Slater [130] uses the general expression (4.2) for the rate constant in the classical approximation, but replaces the classical distribution function by the Wigner distribution function. This approach will obviously give a rate constant at low pressures which is not characterized by a temperature dependence of the Arrhenius type.

In order to eliminate the unnecessary correction for tunneling processes in decomposition reactions at low pressures it is easiest to start from Eq. (2.7), making a separate calculation of the mean lifetime for a system of quantized harmonic oscillators. Such a calculation for a model system of oscillators for which the frequency differences $\Delta\omega_i$ are small in comparison with the mean frequency ω gives the expression [100]

$$\langle\tau\rangle = (v)^{-1}\,(4\pi E_0\,/\,\hbar\omega)^{\frac{s-1}{2}}\,\mu_1\ldots\mu_s, \tag{8.4}$$

where the coefficients μ_i have the same meaning as in the classical model (4.3). The following formula is then obtained for the rate of bimolecular decomposition when $\theta\gg1$:

$$\kappa_0 = Z\left(\frac{4\pi E_0}{\hbar\omega}\right)^{\frac{s-1}{2}}\mu_1\ldots\mu_s\,\exp\left(-\,E_0/kT\right). \tag{8.5}$$

This expression differs from its classical analog by the substitution of $\hbar\omega$ for kT in the pre-exponential term.

9. THE QUASI-EQUILIBRIUM THEORY OF UNIMOLECULAR REACTIONS

The general statistical theory of unimolecular reactions which has been developed in recent years by a number of authors [93, 94, 115, 120, 121, 144] is based, as is Kassel's theory, on the assumption that the total energy in the active molecule can be statistically redistributed over several degrees of freedom, which may be referred to as the active degrees of freedom. However, there are degrees of freedom which do not participate in the activation process (for example, rotation of the molecule as a whole) and which therefore do not contribute to the statistical weight of the vibrationally excited molecule (the adiabatic degrees of freedom). In addition, Marcus has introduced the concept of inactive degrees of freedom, which do not participate in the activation process but can take part in energy exchange in the activated complex. In fact, for a complex molecule such a division of the degrees of freedom is extremely difficult to carry out, since to a considerable extent the intramolecular interactions are unknown. Therefore, in the interpretation of experimental data the possibility of such a division is often used in order to obtain the best agreement with theory.

In comparison with Kassel's theory, the general statistical theory permits several important refinements: the frequency factor $\tilde{\nu}$ can be explicitly evaluated on the basis of the properties of the molecule and the activated complex, derivation of the density of the vibrational spectrum can be based on a more realistic model of a system of harmonic oscillators of various frequencies,* and the effect of anharmonicity and internal rotation on the density of the vibrational levels can be derived.

Calculation of the frequency factor. In evaluating the frequency factor Rosenstock, Wallenstein, Wahrhaftig and Eyring [120], Marcus and Rice [93] as well as Rice [115] started with the assumption that decomposition corresponds to a certain configuration which can be described by the critical coordinate q_0 and the conjugate momentum p. Let $\rho(E)$ denote the density of vibrational levels (in fact all the active degrees of freedom can be included) of an active molecule with an energy E and let $\rho*(E, E_0, E_t)$ denote the density of vibrational levels in an activated molecule, with the same total energy E, close to the critical configuration, which has the potential energy E_0, and possesses a kinetic energy E_t corresponding to a momentum p. Since the assumption of the equiprobable distribution of energy implies that the concentration of activated molecules at a given

---

*Ed. Note: This refinement has also been treated by Kassel, J. Phys. Chem., 32, 1065 (1928).

point in phase space is proportional to the corresponding sta-tistical weight, the following expression can be written for the number of molecules close to the critical configuration:

$$dN = \rho^* (E, E_0, E_t) \, dE \, dp \, dq \, / \, 2\pi\hbar. \tag{9.1}$$

From this it follows, by analogy with the discussion in Section 6, that

$$\frac{dN}{dt} = \frac{1}{2\pi\hbar} \, \rho^* (E, E_0, E_t) \, dE \, dE_t. \tag{9.2}$$

Since it is assumed that the active and activated molecules are in equilibrium, the decomposition rate of the active molecules can be expressed in the form*

$$\varkappa (E) = \frac{1}{2\pi\hbar} \int_0^{E-E_0} \frac{\rho^* (E, E_0, E_t)}{\rho (E)} \, dE_t, \tag{9.3}$$

where integration with respect to dE_t takes into account the de-composition of all excited molecules for which $E_t > 0$. Since the functions $\rho(E)$ and $\rho^*(E, E_0, E_t)$ are determined mainly by the spectral characteristics of the active and activated molecules, the frequency factor will obviously also be determined by these characteristics. It will be clear that this theory does not take into account nonadiabatic and tunneling processes. Moreover, an important limitation is imposed by the assumption that it is pos-sible to separate a reaction coordinate, since the dimensions of the region in which this separation is valid must satisfy the con-dition of quasi-classical motion along the coordinate q. Calcula-tions for certain specific reactions have shown that such a separation is in practice impossible [78].

Calculation of the density of energy levels. For calculation of the density of the energy spectrum, $\rho(E)$ and $\rho^*(E, E_0, E_t)$, it is

---

*Ed. Note: Equation (9.3) follows directly from Eq. (6.1) by recognizing that (6.1) is a rate per unit activated molecule. By changing this to a rate per unit active mole-cule, the indicated ratio of energy level densities arises.

convenient to introduce two new functions $W(E)$ and $W^*(E)$ which give the total number of levels below the level E. Then, obviously

$$\rho(E) = \frac{d}{dE} W(E); \quad \rho^*(E, E_0, E_t) = \frac{d}{dE} W^*(E, E_0, E_t). \quad (9.4)$$

To derive $W(E)$ for a system of harmonic oscillators of various frequencies the following approach, due to Vestal, Wahrhaftig, and Johnston, can be used. It should first be noted that the number of states (or the phase space volume) of a system of s identical oscillators which contains k vibrational quanta is given by

$$W(k) = (s + k)! / s! \, k! \quad (9.5)$$

Therefore, Eq. (7.1) is obtained from evaluating the epxression $g_s(k) = W_s(k) - W_s(k - 1)$, since the differentiation in Eq. (9.4) must here be interpreted as a determination of a finite difference. (See also the remarks following Eq. (9.16) below.) The entire phase space volume can be divided into partial volumes φ_p, each of which corresponds to the excitation of only p oscillators. This division is of the form

$$W(k) = \sum_p \binom{s}{p} \varphi_p(k), \quad (9.6)$$

where

$$\varphi_p(k) = k! / p! \, (k - p)! \quad (9.7)$$

Expression (9.6) can be used for an approximate determination of the phase space volume $W(E)$ of nonidentical oscillators if they are combined into groups characterized by a frequency v_p which is the mean frequency for the group of p oscillators. The introduction of a mean frequency v_p or a mean vibrational quantum $\hbar\omega_p$ means that the number of quanta in each group k_p must be different, since $k_p \hbar\omega_p = E$.

It has been shown [144] that it can be assumed with sufficient accuracy that $k_p = k\sigma_p$, where σ_p is defined in terms of the geometrical mean frequency $\tilde{v}$ of the system of s oscillators and of the normal frequencies v_i:

$$\sigma_p = \sum_{i,\,j\ldots\,l} \left(\frac{\tilde{v}}{v_i} \cdot \frac{\tilde{v}}{v_j} \cdots \frac{\tilde{v}}{v_l} \right)^{1/p}, \tag{9.8}$$

the summation being carried out over all the groups of p oscillators. For an approximate determination of W, the coefficients σ_p can be obtained by a simpler method than the summation of Eq. (9.8) and the functions φ_p can be approximately expressed in the form

$$\varphi_p(k_p) = \left[k\sigma_p - \frac{1}{2}(p-1) \right]^p / p! \tag{9.9}$$

Therefore,

$$W(E) = \sum_p \binom{s}{p} \frac{1}{p!} \left[\frac{E\sigma_p}{\hbar\tilde{\omega}} - \frac{p-1}{2} \right]^p, \tag{9.10}$$

where the summation is carried out from 0 to s if all terms within the square brackets are positive; otherwise the summation is ended with the last positive term. If this summation rule is followed, Eq. (9.10) is an excellent interpolational formula and is valid even at low energies, when the approximation of φ_p by functions of the type (9.9) is not justified.*

As an example we may cite the calculation of $W(E)$ for a model system of 27 harmonic oscillators (8 with a frequency of $(1/3)\tilde{v}$, 11 with a frequency of $\tilde{v}$, and 8 with a frequency of $3\tilde{v}$) which

---

*Lin and Eyring [90a] and Thiele [141a] have proposed a slightly different approach to the determination of $W(E)$ which makes possible a clearer interpretation of the effect of each normal vibration on the phase space volume of a system of s oscillators of various frequencies. **

**Ed. Note: A more complete list might include P. C. Haarhoff, Mol. Physics 6, 337 (1963); 7, 101 (1963); B. S. Rabinovitch et al., J. Chem. Phys. 30, 735 (1959); ibid., 38, 2466 (1963); and E. W. Schlag et al., ibid., 37, 168 (1962); J. Phys. Chem. 69, 1431 (1965).

approximately describes the distribution of frequencies of propane [144]. As the energy increases from 0 to 15 $\hbar\tilde{\omega}$, the true value of W increases from 1 to $3\cdot10^{12}$ and the corresponding values calculated by Eq. (9.10) are 1 to $2.95\cdot10^{12}$ (i.e., the difference is less than 2%). However, the values obtained for W within the limits of the Kassel model employing identical harmonic oscillators only differ from the true values by more than an order of magnitude at high energies [144].

In the limiting case when the number of quanta is much greater than the number of oscillators, each of the brackets in Eq. (9.10) can be expanded as a series in p/k_p and then summed, retaining the largest terms in each of the series of the expansion. In this way the so-called semi-classical Marcus and Rice approximation is obtained [93]:

$$W_{\text{semi-cl}}(E) = \frac{1}{s!}\left[\frac{E+E_z}{\hbar\tilde{\omega}}\right]^s, \qquad (9.11)$$

where E_z is the total energy of the zero-point vibrations. This approximation has been improved by Rabinovitch and Diesen [107] by the introduction of a semi-empirical factor a in front of the term E_z. The factor a has been calculated by Whitten and Rabinovitch [145] for a large number of model molecules by comparing the semi-classical approximation for (9.10) with the results of a direct calculation of the total number of vibrational levels. Although the conditions for the validity of the semi-classical approximation which sets $a = 1$ are not fulfilled for the many reactions involving thermal decompositions and the majority of reactions which involve electron or ion impact in electronically excited states, $W(E)$ can be evaluated without great difficulty by the method given in [145] by a suitable choice of the model and a corresponding selection of a.

In a number of cases it is impossible to represent the spectrum by a small set of groups of identical frequency. Evaluation of the coefficients is then particularly difficult and it is more reasonable to calculate the function $W(E)$ directly for a large number of different frequencies. Several calculations of this type, carried out by means of computers, have been reported and the accuracy of the values obtained for $W(E)$ is of the order of 10%.*

The next problem to be considered is the relationship between the rate of decomposition close to the threshold and the energy excess $E - E_0$. This question is of importance, for example, in evaluating the lifetime of vibrationally excited ions with energies close to the decomposition threshold or in estimating the lifetime of the complex formed by the bimolecular association of polyatomic molecules or radicals. Equation (3.5), the classical expression for the lifetime (which must be equated to the reciprocal of the rate of decomposition) is obtained from the preceding formulas under the condition that $(E - E_0)/\hbar\widetilde{\omega} \gg s$. Despite the fact that this condition is not fulfilled in the majority of cases which are of interest kinetically, Eq. (3.5) is frequently used in calculations (see, for example, [66]). The quantum-mechanical calculation gives considerably shorter values for lifetimes than the classical approach. For example, Wolfsberg [155] has shown that even in the threshold region (energy excess less than 0.1 ev) the lifetime of the $C_3H_8^+$ ion relative to decomposition into $C_3H_7^+$ and H is 10^{-10} seconds, although the classical calculation gives a value three to four orders of magnitude longer. The behavior of the decomposition rate close to the threshold is illustrated in

---

*Such computations have recently been shown to be readily accomplished without this inaccuracy for as many as 100 nonequal harmonic oscillators. Cf. J. Phys. Chem. 69, 1431 (1965) and Refs. [125], [141a].

Fig. 4, in which the abscissa is the excess energy in units of the mean vibrational quantum and the ordinate is the rate of decomposition. The calculation is based on the above model system of 27 oscillators for a frequency $\tilde{v} = 3 \cdot 10^{13}$ sec^{-1}. The solid curve represents the quantum calculation while the dashed curves are based on the classical formula (3.5) with effective numbers of oscillators in the activated molecule $(s - 1)$ of 6, 13, and 26 (curves 1-3).

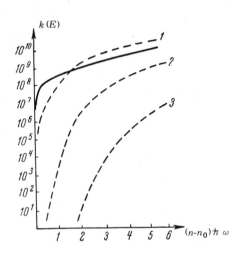

FIG. 4. Relationship between decomposition rate constant $\kappa(E)$ (in sec^{-1}) and excess energy.

The effect of anharmonicity and rotational active degrees of freedom. The effect of anharmonicity on the distribution of the vibrational levels in a complex molecule is twofold: it increases the density of the levels at high excitation energies in comparison with the harmonic oscillator model by reducing the size of the quanta and, in addition, it imposes a restriction on the permissible excitation energy of a single oscillator. These effects have been little investigated, but certain qualitative conclusions can be drawn. The limitations imposed by the finite energy capacity of the oscillators are comparatively unimportant at low energies. Thus, for cyclopropane, when $E < 200$ kcal/mole the correction for this effect changes the phase space volume by less than 1% [143, 125]. An appreciable difference is obtained only when the total energy E is close to the sum of the energies of all the bonds; in this case, however, a statistical description of the process of decomposition is not valid due to the extremely short lifetime of the excited molecule (of the order of several periods of oscillation of the nuclei). For thermal decompositions, when the proportion of molecules with large energies is usually very small, this correction can be neglected.

The effect of anharmonicity on the density of the levels is more important: for cyclopropane, at energies of 10-20 kcal/mole the effect of anharmonicity is very slight, at 150 kcal/mole the phase space volume of a system of anharmonic oscillators differs from the corresponding volume for harmonic oscillators by an order of magnitude, and at 200 kcal/mole by two orders of magnitude [125].* For thermal decomposition reactions the increase in density of the vibrational levels due to anharmonicity causes an increase (relative to the harmonic model) in the rate constant. The rate constant becomes several times greater in the case of triatomic molecules [115] but for polyatomic molecules the change is relatively small (several percent) [125a].

The effect of rotational active degrees of freedom can be estimated relatively simply if the interaction between vibrations and internal rotation is neglected. In this approximation the statistical weights P_r and P_v of the rotational and vibrational degrees of freedom are independent and therefore the density of the energy levels $\rho(E)$ is given by the expression

---

*Ed. Note: For a more recent evaluation of anharmonic effects see J. Chem. Phys. 40, 1461 (1964).

$$\rho\,(E) = \Sigma\,P_r\,(E_r)\,P_v\,(E_v)\,/\,\Delta E,$$
$$E \leqslant E_v + E_r \leqslant E + \Delta E,$$

(9.12)

where the statistical weight of the rotational states $P_r\,(E_r)$ is equal to the product of the statistical weights of the independent internal rotations

$$P_r\,(E_r) = \prod_i P_{r_i}\,(E_{r_i}), \quad P_{r_i} = \begin{cases} 2J_i + 1 & \text{for a two-dimensional rotator} \\ 2 & \text{for a one-dimensional rotator} \end{cases}$$

(9.13)

Since, for the majority of cases, internal rotation in molecules can be assumed to be quasi-classical, the summation in Eq. (9.12) over the rotational quantum numbers J_i can be replaced by integration, using the relationship between energy and momentum

$$E_r = \hbar^2 J\,(J + 1)\,/\,2I_r.$$

The following expression is then obtained for $\rho\,(E)$:

$$\rho\,(E) = \Sigma P_v\,(E_v)\frac{1}{\Delta E} \int_{\Delta E} \prod_i 2\,(J_i)^{d_i-1}dJ_i = \left(\frac{2}{\hbar^2}\right)^{r/2} \times$$
$$\times \frac{\prod_i (I_i)^{d_i/2}\,\Gamma\left(\frac{d_i}{2}\right)}{\Gamma\left(\frac{r}{2}\right)} \sum_{E_v < E} P_v\,(E_v)\,(E - E_v)^{\frac{r}{2}-1},$$

(9.14)

where $r = \sum\limits_i d_i$ is the total number of degrees of freedom for internal rotation. In this expression it is convenient to replace the moments of inertia of internal rotation I_i by the corresponding partition functions. In this way the expression

$$\rho\,(E) = \frac{F_r}{(kT)^{r/2}\,\Gamma\,(r\,/\,2)} \sum_{E_v=0}^{E} P_v\,(E_v)\,(E - E_v)^{\frac{r}{2}-1}$$

(9.15)

is obtained, where F_r is the total partition function for internal rotations. Although kT appears in this expression explicitly, the density $\rho(E)$ is in fact independent of temperature, since F_r contains the factor $(kT)^{r/2}$ implicitly. If there is no free internal rotation in the active molecule, r must be set equal to zero in the above expressions. Formula (9.15) then becomes indeterminate, since both the numerator (when $E^{\cdot} = E_0$) and the denominator (as a result of the multiplier $\Gamma(0)$) become infinite. Removal of the indeterminacy leads to the expected result

$$\rho(E)\big|_{r=0} = P(E_v)\big|_{E=E_v}. \tag{9.16}$$

In connection with the above equation and also with Eq. (9.10), the following comment must be made. Strictly speaking, for a quantized model of a stable molecule the function $W = W(E)$ is of a stepwise nature and the function $\rho(E)$ contains a delta function. These peculiarities disappear when the energy region of the activated molecule is considered. As a result of the quasi-stationary character of the quantum state of the actived molecule the energy levels widen, and Rice has shown [115] that this widening is of the order of magnitude necessary to smooth the function $W(E)$. Thus, $W(E)$ in Eq. (9.10) must be considered to be a continuous function of E. The function $\rho(E)$ in Eq. (9.14) must be understood to represent the density of the vibrational levels averaged over an energy interval δE which is greater than the distance between the levels but small in comparison with the width of the energy distribution of the active molecule $\overline{\Delta E}$.

However, cases may occur in which smoothing of $W(E)$ and $\rho(E)$ is impossible. The discrete structure of the vibrational spectrum can obviously only be observed if the width Γ_λ of the energy level E_λ is small in comparison with the distance between neighboring levels $\Delta E_{\lambda\lambda'}$, which must in turn be greater than $\overline{\Delta E}$ (for thermal reactions obviously $\overline{\Delta E} \approx kT$). Such relationships between Γ_λ, $\Delta E_{\lambda\lambda'}$, and $\overline{\Delta E}$ are quite possible for nonadiabatic reactions [5, 23].

Integrating Eq. (9.2) over all energies of the reaction coordinate E_t, in accordance with the definition of $\kappa(E)$, leads to the following expression for the rate constant (the intermediate steps, which are analogous to those in the derivation of Eq. (9.14), have been omitted):

$$\kappa(E) = F_1^+ N^+(E) / 2\pi\hbar F_1 \rho(E), \qquad (9.17)$$

where F_1^+ / F_1 is the ratio of the partition functions of the adiabatic degrees of freedom of the activated and active molecules, $\rho(E)$ is given by Eq. (9.15), and $N^+(E)$ is of the form

$$N^+(E) = \frac{F_r^+}{(kT)^{q/2} \Gamma\left(\frac{q}{2}+1\right)} \sum_{E_v^+=0}^{E^+} P_v^+(E_v^+)(E^+ - E_v^+)^{q/2}, \qquad (9.18)$$

where q is the number of internal rotational degrees of freedom of the activated molecule and E^+, the energy of the activated molecule, is equal to $E - E_0 - E_z$. In the simplest case of a molecule which is represented by a system of s harmonic oscillators of identical frequency ω, the values to be substituted into Eqs. (9.15) and (9.18) are $r = q = 0$, $P_v(E_n) = (n + s - 1)! / (s - 1)! \, n!$, $P_v^+(E_n^+) = (\Delta n + s - 2)! / \Delta n! \, (s - 2)!$, $\Delta n = n - n_0$. Evaluating the sum in Eq. (9.18), we get

$$\kappa(E_n) = \nu \frac{(\Delta n + s - 1)! \, n!}{(n + s - 1)! \, \Delta n!}. \qquad (9.19)$$

This expression can be used for evaluation of the lifetime of an active molecule, $\langle \tau(E) \rangle = 1/\kappa(E)$, both close $(\Delta n < s - 1)$ to and far $(\Delta n \gg s - 1)$ from the threshold.

Generalization of the theory of quasi-stationary unimolecular reactions to derive results which are valid at any pressure is based on the assumption of random distribution of the lifetime of the active molecule and the mechanism of strong activating collisions. By a process which is completely analogous to the derivation of Eq. (2.9) we obtain the following expression:

$$\kappa = \alpha \frac{kT}{2\pi\hbar} \frac{F_r^+ F_2^+}{F_1 F_2} \frac{\exp(-E_0/kT)}{(r/2)!} \times$$

$$\times \int_0^\infty \sum_{E_v^+ \leqslant E^+} \frac{P_v^+(E_v^+)(E^+ - E_v^+)^{r/2} \exp(-E^+/kT)}{1 + \kappa_a/Z} dE^+, \tag{9.20}$$

$$\kappa_a = \alpha \frac{F_1^+}{F_1} \frac{F_r^+}{2\pi\hbar} \frac{1}{(r/2)!} \sum_{E_v^+ \leqslant E^+} \frac{P_v^+(E_v^+)[(E^+ - E_v^+)/kT]^{r/2}}{\rho(E_0 + E_r + E^+)},$$

where α is the symmetry number of the activated molecule,* F_1 and F_1^+ are the partition functions of the adiabatic degrees of freedom on the active and activated molecules, respectively. F_2 is the partition function of all the active degrees of freedom, and F_r^+ is the partition function of active rotations. The following expressions for the rate constant in the limiting cases of high and low pressure are obtained from (9.20):

$$\kappa_\infty = \frac{kT}{2\pi\hbar} \frac{F_1^+ F_2^+}{F_1 F_2} \exp(-E_0/kT), \tag{9.21}$$

$$\kappa_0 = Z \frac{F_2^{cl}}{F_2^{qu}} \left(\frac{E_0 + E_z}{kT}\right)^{s + \frac{r}{2} - 1} \exp(-E_0/kT) / \Gamma\left(s + \frac{r}{2}\right), \tag{9.22}$$

where F_2^{cl} and F_2^{qu} denote the partition functions of all the active degrees of freedom calculated for the classical and quantum models, respectively.

---

*Ed. Note: This assumes that all symmetry numbers have been factored from the corresponding rotational partition functions and are combined in α. Further kinetic factors may also appear (see J. Chem. Phys. 42, 584 (1965)).

The isotope effect. One of the interesting consequences of quantum theories of unimolecular reactions is the prediction of various isotope effects, which consist in a variation of the rate constant of a reaction caused by changes in the isotopic composition of the molecules.

The appearance of the isotope effect in classical theories of unimolecular reaction is due to the fact that the frequency factor of the rate constant at high pressures depends on the mass of the atoms. The relationship between the frequency factor and the mass of the atoms is, generally speaking, extremely complex, since the reaction coordinate is related to the motion of all the atoms of the molecule. However, for the classical harmonic model it can be shown that if the reaction coordinate corresponds to the breaking of a bond between atoms A and B, the ratio of the frequency factors $\tilde{\nu}'/\tilde{\nu}$ for the isotopic substitutions $A \to A'$ and $B \to B'$ is $(M_{AB}/M_{A'B'})^{1/2}$ [130]. Thus, an increase in the mass of A and B causes a decrease in the pre-exponential factor. If the quantization of the vibrations and its effect on the rate of decomposition under equilibrium conditions are taken into account, it is found that, in addition to the frequency factor, the effective energy of dissociation is changed by isotopic substitution. This is due to the fact that the energy of the zero-point vibrations depends on the mass of the atoms. Since this energy decreases with increasing atomic mass, the effective dissociation energy, which is equal to the difference between the energies of the initial and final molecules, in general increases with increasing atomic mass, and thus the rate of decomposition of molecules with light isotopes will be greater than that of similar molecules with heavy isotopes. These effects are known as the normal primary isotope effects.

Under nonequilibrium conditions, changes in the masses of the atoms affect not only the activation energy and the frequency factor, but also the density of the energy levels of the active molecule. Consider, for example, the decomposition of molecules with an initial vibrational distribution according to a δ-function. On the basis of Eqs. (9.15) and (9.16) the rate constant can be written in the form (for simplicity the partition functions of the adiabatic degrees of freedom have been omitted and it has been assumed that internal rotation is absent):

$$\varkappa(E) = \frac{1}{2\pi\hbar} \sum_{E_v^+ < E - E_0} P_v^+(E_v^+) \Big/ \rho^*(E), \qquad (9.23)$$

where $E - E_0$ is the excess of energy above the threshold. In the limit as $E \to E_0$, $P_v^+ \to 1$ and the ratio of the rate constants for light and heavy molecules is inversely proportional to the density of the vibrational levels close to the threshold. Since the density of the vibrational levels is greater for a heavy molecule than for a light molecule, the rate of decomposition will be lower for the heavy molecule. This is known as the normal secondary isotope effect.

However, for thermal decomposition at low pressures, which is also characterized by intense disturbance of the equilibrium distribution, an increase in density of the vibrational levels close to the threshold under the condition $\hbar\omega \gg kT$ increases the rate of decomposition and leads to the inverse secondary isotope effect.

Although experimental isolation of any one of the isotope effects is extremely difficult, these effects have been detected in various nonequilibrium systems [59, 60, 63, 108].

10. THE EFFECT OF VARIOUS DEGREES OF FREEDOM ON THE RATE OF SPONTANEOUS DECOMPOSITION

Slater's harmonic model. For Slater's harmonic model the mean lifetime is given by Eqs. (4.5) and (8.4). The first equation is applicable to the classical case under the condition $E - E_0 \gg \hbar \omega s$, that is, for excitation energies which are sufficiently far from the threshold. The second equation is applicable to calculation of the lifetime of a system of almost identical harmonic oscillators close to the threshold under the condition $E - E_0 \leqslant \hbar \omega$. As was noted above, Eqs. (4.5) and (8.4) clearly show that the reduction of the interaction between the reaction coordinate and the normal coordinates Q_j, which is reflected in a decrease in the reduced amplitude factors μ_j, causes a decrease in the lifetime of the active molecule. In particular, it can happen that certain of the coefficients μ_j vanish. They must then be omitted from Eqs. (4.5) and (8.4), with a corresponding reduction in the number of vibrational degrees of freedom s. In the classical case such an effective decrease in the vibrational degrees of freedom can be considered to be the result of complete nonparticipation of certain of the normal vibrations in the intramolecular energy transfer.

In the quantum case, as has been shown in [23], the effective decrease in vibrational degrees of freedom must be interpreted as a consequence of the nonparticipation in intramolecular energy exchange of those excited vibrational configurations for which part of the excitation energy is concentrated on normal vibrations which are ineffective in the classical case (configuration is here understood to mean some distribution of the vibrational quantum numbers over noninteracting quantum oscillators, each of which represents a normal vibration of the molecule). It should, finally, be noted that if there is a group of p degenerate vibrations in the molecule, the effect of these vibrations will be equal to the effect of a single vibration with an amplitude factor given by

$$\mu^2 = \sum_p \mu_p^2.$$

Consider, for example, a linear triatomic molecule. It will be assumed that the frequencies of all four normal vibrations (two valency vibrations and one doubly-degenerate deformation) are almost identical. If the activated state is not axially symmetrical, both the valency and the deformational vibrations will contribute to the mean lifetime. Since, however, the deformational vibration is doubly-degenerate, it must be assumed that $s = 3$ and not that $s = 4$. If the activated state is axially symmetrical, the deformation will not interact with the reaction coordinate, and therefore $s = 2$. This implies that only configurations of the type $\sigma_1^{n_1}\sigma_2^{n_2}$ participate in the resolution of the wave function of the activated molecule into the wave functions of the vibrationally-excited active molecule. Configurations of the type $\sigma_1^{n_1}\sigma_2^{n_2}\pi^{n_3}$ will not take part in this resolution. Here σ_1, σ_2, and π denote vibrational functions of valency and deformational vibrations, and the numbers n_1, n_2 and n_3 are related to the total number of excited quanta in the molecule n by the equation $n_1 + n_2 + n_3 = n.$

Kassel's model. In interpreting experimental values of thermal decomposition rate constants or lifetimes of vibrationally excited ions it is often necessary to treat s as an empirical factor which denotes the number of harmonic oscillators which effectively participate in intramolecular energy exchange [7], and it is found that s_{eff} is only a certain fraction of the total number of degrees of freedom. This leads to an extremely indefinite physical picture of energy exchange, since it must be assumed that the coupling between some of the oscillators and the reaction coordinate (which in principle is not zero even in the harmonic approximation) is less than the anharmonic coupling between the active oscillators among which the statistical redistribution of energy occurs. The difference between s and s_{eff} is at present ascribed mainly to the incorrect use of the classical theory for the interpretation of the results of experiments for which the conditions of applicability of this classical theory ($\hbar\omega_i \ll kT$ for thermal decomposition and $E - E_0 \gg \hbar\omega s$ for the decomposition of ions in a mass spectrometer) are not fulfilled. Within the limits of Kassel's model there are no vibrationally-excited configurations which can be excluded when considering intramolecular energy transfer, since such an exclusion contradicts the basis of the model. However, if the activated state has a certain symmetry, complete wave functions of the vibrationally excited molecule which take into account anharmonic coupling between the oscillators but which correspond to different types of symmetry cannot hybridize as a result of intramolecular interaction. Formally, this effect can appear as a decrease in the effective number of the degrees of freedom.*

To clarify this, consider the model of a linear triatomic molecule discussed above. If the activated state is axially symmetrical, the complete wave functions of the active and activated molecules will correspond to definite values of the projection of the vibrational moment on the symmetry axis. This means that in the most general form the wave function of the activated molecule must be resolvable into functions of all the configurations of the

---

*Ed. Note: See also Laidler and Wojciechowski and discussion thereof in *The Transition State*, Special Publication No. 16, Chemical Society, London (1962).

harmonic approximation; however, from any configuration, which in general will be multiply degenerate, only those terms which correspond to one and the same projection of the vibrational moment will be involved. For the lifetime $\langle \tau \rangle$ of the lower Σ^+ state of the active triatomic molecule the expression $\langle \tau \rangle = (\tilde{\nu})^{-1} n_0^2/4$ can be obtained [100], where $n_0 = E_0/\hbar\omega$. For the same model, Slater's theory gives $\langle \tau \rangle = (\tilde{\nu})^{-1}(\pi n_0)^{1/2}$. If it is assumed that the energy can be statistically redistributed between all the states of the active molecule and not only between states with identical moments, the corresponding expression would be $\langle \tau \rangle = (\tilde{\nu})^{-1} n_0^3/3!$. It will be seen that the absence of interaction between terms with different symmetries can formally be considered as a reduction of the effective number of oscillators, but it is not possible to indicate any definite types of oscillator which do not interact with the reaction coordinate. It should be noted that the interaction of terms with different symmetries implies the existence of a sufficiently intense vibrational-rotational interaction, since only in this case does the vibrational moment loose the significance of a precise quantum number. The analogous question of the exclusion of nonactive degrees of freedom in the classical case has been discussed by Slater [133].

The quasi-equilibrium theory of unimolecular reactions. In the quasi-equilibrium theory of unimolecular reactions all vibrations and internal rotations are considered as active degrees of freedom. This theory claims to take into account the possibility of the transformation of one type of motion in the active molecule into another type of motion in the activated molecule (for example, the conversion of free rotation with respect to the C — C bond in vibrationally highly-excited ions and molecules of saturated hydrocarbons into torsional oscillations with respect to the same bond in the activated molecules [121]). At the same time, in evaluating the density of the energy levels the theory assumes that it is possible to distinguish (although only approximately) vibrations and internal rotations. It is clear that interconversion of different types of motion must be related to very great anharmonic interactions of the vibrational and rotational degrees of freedom with the reaction coordinate. Therefore, it is difficult to decide definitely to what extent the assumptions of the possibility of distinguishing between the various degrees of freedom and of the implicit allowance for great anharmonicity are compatible in the evaluation of the density of the energy levels. Degrees of freedom which correspond to rotation of the molecule as a whole are usually considered to be adiabatic [121]. Two effects caused by rotation of the decomposing molecule can be indicated qualitatively. First, centrifugal force reduces the effective dissociation energy. This reduction, which is analogous to the corresponding effect for diatomic molecules [98], can be evaluated if it is assumed that internal motions of the molecule can be separated from rotation of the molecule as a whole. In addition, rotation of the molecule considerably increases the anharmonicity of vibrations and leads to an increase in the rate of energy exchange between the various degrees of freedom. Second, rotation of the molecule interacts dynamically with internal motions. This interaction may either very slightly change the density of the energy levels of the active molecule and thus merely cause interaction of terms with different symmetries (as was observed in the model of the linear triatomic molecule considered above), or it may fundamentally alter the energy spectrum of the active molecule. In the latter case the effect of rotation on the reaction rate will not be adiabatic and therefore it will not be possible to correct the effect by the introduction of a multiplier F_1^+ into the expression for the rate constant of decomposition. An approximate correction for the effect of rotation can be made if the corresponding degrees of freedom are treated as active. The existence of such an intense rotational effect is apparently indicated by the results of certain experimental investigations.

11. NONADIABATIC REACTIONS

The classical and quantum theories of unimolecular reactions considered above all deal with adiabatic reactions, for which it may, with sufficient accuracy, be assumed that there is a definite potential which determines the motion (classical or quantized) of the representative point in phase space. This potential is evaluated as the electronic energy of the system of atoms which form the molecule for fixed values of the nuclear coordinates. Since, however, the energy of the electronic terms depends on the electronic quantum numbers, there is always a wide choice of such potentials or potential energy surfaces, motion along which corresponds to one of the possible adiabatic processes. Motion of the nuclei can, in principle, lead to transition between potential surfaces, such transition in general occurring in regions where surfaces converge or intersect. If a reaction pathway includes a transition between potential energy surfaces at some point, the reaction is said to be nonadiabatic. By this definition, all reactions which could in principle proceed by an infinitely slow change of the coordinates of the nuclei must be considered adiabatic. However, discussions of transitions between various electronic terms frequently take into account terms which are based not only on the adiabatic approximation, but also on a number of other approximations. With such an imprecise definition of the concept of adiabatic electronic terms it may happen that transitions between terms are caused not only by dynamic interaction between the electrons and nuclei, but also by static interactions which have not been taken into account in calculating the terms. Consider, for example, rupture of the N — O bond in the N_2O molecule. The shape of the potential curve is shown qualitatively in Fig. 5. As a result of dissociation, the linear N_2O molecule

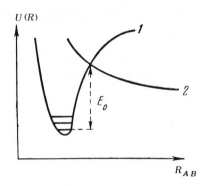

FIG. 5. Potential curves for non-adiabatic reaction (predissociation).

undergoes a transition from the $^1\Sigma$ state to the $^1\Sigma$ and ^3P states of the N_2 molecule and the O atom. It is usually assumed here that the change in the multiplicity of the term occurs close to the point of intersection of the terms of the stable $^1\Sigma$ state (term 1) and unstable $^3\Pi$ state (term 2) of the N_2O molecule. This process is considered to be nonadiabatic since the reaction produces a change in the multiplicity and, consequently, in the electronic quantum numbers of the molecule. However, if spin–orbit interaction is taken into account, the electronic terms cannot be characterized by a definite spin value. In the case under consideration

the terms can be characterized with any degree of accuracy by
definite spin values only when they are far from the point of
quasi-intersection of the $^1\Sigma'$ and $^3\Pi$ curves. Indeed, it is only
when the spin-orbit interaction is small that it can be considered
as the cause of the change in the multiplicity of the term during
transition from the initial state of the system (equilibrium inter-
nuclear states of N_2O ($^1\Sigma$)) to the final state (a free oxygen atom
(^3P) and a nitrogen molecule ($^1\Sigma$)). The cause of true nonadiabatic
transition between terms of Σ and Π symmetries of a linear triatomic molecule might be (if the multiplicities of the terms were
equal) the interaction of the molecular rotation with the electronic
angular momentum. If there is strong spin-orbit interaction it
must, of course, be taken into account in evaluating the adiabatic
electronic terms even in the zero-order approximation. In the
above example of the N_2O molecule, the spin-orbit interaction
could also have been included from the start in the calculation of
the adiabatic terms. Then, the projection of the total moment Ω
(spin and mechanical) onto the axis of the molecule would have
been selected as the electronic quantum number, and decomposition of the N_2O molecule could have been considered as a typical
adiabatic process proceeding without any change in the electronic
state characterized by a quantum number $\Omega = 0$. This confusion
in the definition of nonadiabatic transitions and reactions which
has become established in the literature must always be borne in
mind [7].

Hereafter we shall consider only such cases in which the
spin-orbit interaction is slight and adiabatic terms will be
understood to refer to those electronic states which are characterized by definite values of the total electronic spin. In these
cases, spin-orbit interaction as well as dynamic interaction of

the electrons and nuclei must be considered as the cause of non-adiabatic transitions.

The vibrational energy of the active molecule in decomposition reactions is usually so great that transitions into excited electronic states of the molecule are quite possible. The corresponding potential energy surfaces can be classified into three types with respect to the considered reaction. First, it may occur that adiabatic motion along such a surface does not lead to any reaction at all. A molecule AB in such an electronic state m must nevertheless be considered as an active molecule, the probability of its decomposition being determined not only by intramolecular energy transfer but also by the probability of nonadiabatic transition to another surface l which will lead to decomposition. Second, the surface m can correspond to an adiabatic reaction pathway. If the lifetime of the molecule in this electronic state appreciably exceeds the characteristic vibration time of the nuclei, such a molecule must be considered to be active. If, however, the lifetime is of the order of the period of vibration of the nuclei, the corresponding potential energy surface must be classified as a third type, and the molecule must be considered to be activated. The $^3\Pi$ terms in the isoelectronic molecules CO_2 and N_2O provide examples of the last two types of surface. For the CO_2 molecule the $^3\Pi$ excited state apparently corresponds to a relatively deep potential well, and thus the lifetime of the molecule in this state can be quite long. For the N_2O molecule this state is characterized by a wave function which is strongly antibonding with respect to the $N-O$ bond, and thus dissociation of the $N-O$ bond on transition of the nitrous oxide molecule into this state must occur within a time of the order of 10^{-13}–10^{-14} seconds.

Nonadiabatic transitions can, of course, occur when the vibrational energy E is less than the threshold value E_0, and in this case they form part of the activation process. If the rates of such transitions are greater than the rate of vibrational excitation of the reacting molecule during collisions, then such transitions cannot limit the rate of excitation, and thus have practically no effect on the reaction rate. If, however, the rate of nonadiabatic transitions is less than the rate of vibrational excitation, it is quite possible that these transitions will determine the rate of the reaction. Recent experiments on the decomposition of CO_2 behind a shock front [44], in which it was found that the effective dissociation energy (86 kcal/mole) was appreciably lower than the true dissociation energy (126.7 kcal/mole)* have been interpreted from this point of view.

There have as yet been no theoretical investigations of the general theory of nonadiabatic transitions in complex molecules which are vibrationally highly excited. The fundamental difficulty here is that the nonadiabatic transition must be investigated in a multidimensional space, furthermore, the effect of intermolecular collisions on intramolecular transitions (transitions such as in the case of forced predissociation of a diatomic molecule) must be taken into account. Rice [117] and Nikitin [22] have discussed this problem qualitatively in relationship to the dissociation of diatomic molecules. The well-developed theory of nonadiabatic transitions in diatomic molecules can only be used in calculations of the transition probability in those cases in which the complex motion of the representative point in the

---

*It should be noted that this value of the dissociation energy is obtained if the rate constant is expressed in the Arrhenius form, with a temperature-independent pre-exponential factor. The same interpretation of later experiments [95a] gives $E_0 = 99$ kcal/mole.

region of greatest nonadiabatic interaction can be reduced to one-dimensional motion [8].

Consider, for example, transition between terms 1 and 2 in Fig. 5. In calculating the probability of transition it must be noted, above all, that the greatest contribution will be made by those vibrational states of the stable diatomic molecule for which the center of rotation lies close to the point of intersection of the terms. If in this region the wave functions of the nuclei in the electronic states 1 and 2 are approximately represented by Airy functions, the following expression may be obtained for the probability of transition with double crossing of the point R^*[8]:

$$P = \frac{4\pi (W)^2 (2\mu)^{2/3}}{\hbar^{4/3} (F_1 F_2)^{1/3} (\Delta F)^{2/3}} \, \Phi^2 \left[-\Delta E \left(\frac{2\mu}{\hbar^2} \right)^{1/3} \left(\frac{\Delta F}{F_1 F_2} \right)^{2/3} \right], \qquad (11.1)$$

where F_1 and F_2 are the forces acting on the nuclei at the point of intersection R^*, $\Delta F = |F_1 - F_2|$, W is the electronic matrix element of nonadiabatic interaction, and μ is the reduced mass; the energy ΔE is measured from the point of intersection of the terms, i.e., $\Delta E = E - E_0$.

If it is assumed that $\Delta E = 0$ close to the point of intersection, and that the distribution function of the vibrational states is of the Boltzmann type $f(\Delta E)d(\Delta E) = \exp(-\beta^* \Delta E)d(\beta^* \Delta E)$, then, by averaging over this distribution, the following expression is obtained [99]:

$$\langle P \rangle = \frac{2\pi W^2}{\hbar \Delta F} (2\pi \mu \beta^*)^{1/2} \exp [(\beta^*)^3 \, 2\mu \Delta F / 12\hbar^2 F_1 F_2]. \qquad (11.2)$$

The first multiplier in Eq. (11.2) gives the probability of transition in the Landau–Zener approximation. The second multiplier is a correction factor which takes into account tunneling transitions between electronic terms. It will be obvious that $1/k\beta^*$ in this expression is a characteristic of the vibrational distribution of the reacting molecule and that in general it may differ from the temperature T of translational motion of the molecule.

The fundamental defect of a one-dimensional model is that it does not take into account explicitly the interaction of the reaction coordinate with the other degrees of freedom of the active molecule. This interaction can be studied only in relatively simple models. In particular, for the model of strictly harmonic molecular vibrations nonadiabatic transitions, such as in predissociation, along one of the bonds of the molecule, in fact imply predissociation for all the normal vibrations. This in turn leads to the appearance of many points of intersection closely spaced along the energy axis [23]. Nevertheless, it may be assumed that Eq. (11.2) will give the correct order of magnitude for the probability of nonadiabatic transitions.

In order to evaluate $\langle P \rangle$ it may be initially assumed that the effect of tunneling transitions can be neglected and the second multiplier in Eq. (11.2) must then be set equal to unity. In the case of the intersection of the terms shown in Fig. 5, we assume that in the first multiplier $\Delta F \approx F \approx D\alpha$, where D is a quantity of the order of magnitude of the bond energy in the molecule, and $1/\alpha$ is the radius of action of the exchange forces ($0.3 \cdot 10^{-8}$– $0.5 \cdot 10^{-8}$ cm). The effective vibrational temperature $1/k\beta^*$ for nonequilibrium processes may differ from the temperature of translational motion, but for thermal reaction it can be assumed that β^* is approximately equal to $1/kT$. For allowed spin-orbit interactions which cause transition between molecular states with appreciably differing wave functions close to the nuclei of the atoms, the magnitude of W must be of the same order as the spin-orbit coupling constant in the free atoms. A transition of exactly this type exists in the CO_2 molecule, where the change in symmetry of the complete wave function ($^1\Sigma \rightarrow {}^3\Pi$) occurs as the result of a change in the symmetry of the hybridized atomic orbits. In this case $W \approx$ 100-200 cm^{-1}. If this value is substituted into Eq. (11.2) and it is assumed that $T \approx 1000°$K, it is found that the probability of a nonadiabatic transition is of the order of 10^{-1}-10^{-2}, without taking into account the correction for tunneling transitions. If, however, a spin-orbit transition (allowed by general selection rules) connects states whose wave functions differ only in the weights of the atomic orbitals they contain, but the atomic orbitals are themselves not changed in the transition, then the electronic matrix element of spin-orbit interaction may be appreciably smaller than the corresponding atomic constant. Thus, for example, for transitions between lower states of a molecule containing π-electrons (a molecule of the type of benzene) W is approximately 1 cm^{-1}. This indicates a decrease in the probability of transition with respect to the preceding example of four orders of magnitude. This value of $\langle P \rangle \approx 10^{-6}$ is usually used to evaluate the probability of "intercombinational" nonradiative transitions in aromatic molecules [79]. A value of the same order of magnitude is used for the probability of singlet-triplet transitions in *cis-trans* isomerization reactions [2, 91, 95], which were mentioned in the discussion of Slater's theory. Spin-orbit interaction in such molecules is, of course, greatly affected by the replacement of light atoms by heavy ones, and this must always be borne in mind in evaluating the probability of transition in the general case.

For nonadiabatic transitions induced by dynamic interactions between the nuclei and electrons, the matrix element must depend on the velocity of the nuclei and increase as this velocity increases. Thus, for example, for the transition between the Σ and Π terms of a linear molecule which was discussed above, the result of the interaction between the rotation of the nuclei and the electronic moment is that W is approximately equal to the mean energy of a rotational quantum.

The tunneling correction, which is represented by the second multiplier in Eq. (11.2), must now be considered. For atoms with a mean atomic weight $\mu \approx 10$, and with the above-mentioned values of the parameters ΔF, F, D and α, it is found that the exponent is greater than unity when $D\beta^* > 10$. Since for many thermal decomposition reactions this inequality is fulfilled, the result indicates that tunneling transitions may have an effect even when the energy barrier is relatively wide (Fig. 5). Although the linear approximation which is used for the terms near their intersection in the derivation of Eq. (11.2) limits the validity of this formula, it can still happen (even when the formula is valid) that the mean probability of transition is greater than unity as a result of the large value of the exponential multiplier. The inequality $\langle P \rangle > 1$ is related to the normalization of the distribution function and simply indicates the effective lowering of the reaction threshold E_0, which enters exponentially into the expression for the rate constant, $\kappa \approx \langle P \rangle \exp(-\beta^* E_0)$.

The effect of tunneling transitions can be particularly great if the energy barriers are narrow, when the terms diverge only slowly near the point of intersection ($\Delta F \ll F_1, F_2$). In fact, such a parallel disposition of the terms is extremely probable for polyatomic molecules, for which the density of the electronically excited states can be high. In this case it might be possible to characterize the probability of nonradiative tunneling transitions from excited states into the ground state by parameters which describe the mean change in the shape of the potential energy surface on electronic excitation (for example, the change in the mean curvature at the minimum, or the mean square displacement of the minima of the terms of the ground or excited states). This approach to the description of nonadiabatic transitions has been developed by Hunt et al. [73].

It must finally be noted that existing experimental data on the effect of isotopic substitutions on the intensity of phosphorescence of complex molecules indicate the importance of tunneling effects in nonadiabatic transitions [119].

12. COMPARISON OF THEORY WITH EXPERIMENT

Several variants of the classical and quantum theories have been used in attempts to interpret experimental data on unimolecular reactions of polyatomic molecules. In the high pressure region, when the equilibrium distribution of the reacting molecules with respect to the vibrational states is basically undisturbed, the rate constant κ_∞ is a function of two parameters, the frequency factor $\tilde{\nu}$ and the activation energy E_0, if it is assumed in addition that tunneling transitions do not affect the rate of reaction. At the present time E_0 cannot be theoretically predicted with sufficient accuracy, and therefore the activation energy is determined either from the temperature dependence of κ_∞, or from independent experiments. The frequency factor, if it lies in the "normal" range of $10^{13}-10^{14}$ sec^{-1}, can usually be interpreted within the limits of oscillator models of the active molecule. When, however, the frequency factor appreciably exceeds this value the difference between the intramolecular motions in the active and unexcited molecules must be taken into account (cf. Section 6). If $\tilde{\nu}$ is much smaller than $10^{13}-10^{14}$ sec^{-1}, this may be due to the nonadiabatic character of the reaction (cf. Section 11).

If an attempt is made to correct for tunneling transitions within the limits of the Slater model [130], it is found that Eq. (8.3) yields too high a value for transmission under the energy barrier, as should have been expected from the concepts developed in Section 8. Thus, for example, investigation of the isomerization of cyclopropane shows that the observed temperature dependence of the rate constant differs appreciably from that obtained from Eq. (8.3) [132a]. In order to obtain agreement between theory and experiment, the contribution of the zero-point vibrations must be eliminated from σ^2 in Eq. (8.3). This is equivalent to a partial correction for the tunneling effect in Slater's model.

In the intermediate, or low pressure regions the possible validity of one or another variant of the theories depends on the value of the dimensionless parameters E_z/E_0, s and θ. The classical theory of unimolecular reactions is only valid when $\theta \ll 1$. When $\theta \gtrsim 1$, the formulas of the quantum theory must be used. The incorrect application of the classical theory to derive the rate constant under relatively low temperature conditions, when the maximum characteristic temperature of the reacting molecule $\hbar\omega_{max}/k$ is of the order of or greater than the temperature T, can lead to a much too high value for the rate constant and to an incorrect value for the temperature dependence of the pre-exponential factor.

In calculating the density of the states g_s of the active molecule, the principal contribution is usually due to the vibrational degrees of freedom. In this case g_s can be evaluated in the semi-classical approximation (9.11), if the condition $s \ll 6(E_0+E_z)^2/E_z^2$ is fulfilled. If this condition is not fulfilled (for example, for the

N_2O_4 molecule $E_0 \approx 3900$ cm^{-1}, $E_z \approx 5200$ cm^{-1}, and $s = 12$), it is possible that a better approximation for g_s will be given by Eq. (7.1), in which, in evaluating n, the value of ω must represent some mean frequency of the vibrations of the reacting molecule. Such an approximation for g_s will only be satisfactory if the variation of ω close to $\langle \omega \rangle$, as a result of the frequency scatter, leads to a reasonable (from the point of view of comparison with experiment) variation in g_{s^*}. This approach to the calculation of g_s is presented in [98].

Recently, a large number of thermal decomposition and isomerization reactions has been discussed within the framework of the theories considered above. Although these investigations [98, 115, 150] will not be discussed in detail, it must be noted that in the majority of cases Kassel's theory gave a better agreement with the experimental results than did Slater's theory [137] when one considers an evaluation of the rate constant for a given reaction or its pressure dependence. In turn, the quasi-equilibrium theory of unimolecular reactions often makes it possible to improve the value of the rate constant derived on the basis of Kassel's theory. In particular, it gives a more or less precise meaning to the value of the vibrational quantum of the system of identical harmonic oscillators which represents the molecule in Kassel's theory.* Statistical theories enable the correct evaluation of the rate of decomposition or isomerization for a large number of unimolecular reactions under thermal conditions, and provide the means for a qualitative derivation of the effect of a strongly nonequilibrium vibrational distribution on the reaction rate constant.

---

*Ed. Note: Kassel also considered this ramification of his model, cf. J. Phys. Chem. 32, 1065 (1928).

As an illustration of the application of the theories of uni-molecular decomposition and of the difficulties which still have to be overcome in the creation of a complete theory, consider the thermal decomposition of nitrous oxide. The rate constant of this reaction has been determined experimentally in the high and intermediate pressure ranges [77]. The experimental conditions and the effect of various factors on the observed reaction rate have been discussed by Kondrat'yev [7] and Johnston [77]. This reaction was first considered from the point of view of non-adiabatic processes by Stearn and Eyring [134]. These authors found, on the basis of the experimental value of the rate constant at high pressures and the known value of the activation energy which was then accepted to be 52 kcal/mole, that the probability of nonadiabatic transition between the $^1\Sigma^+$ and $^3\Pi$ terms (cf. Section 11) must be of the order of 10^{-4}. Later experiments [77] gave a value for the activation energy $E_0 = 60$ kcal/mole. In this case, as Gill and Laidler have shown [66], the probability of non-adiabatic transition is of the order of 10^{-1}-10^{-2}. This estimate agrees with the general discussion present in Section 11.

The experimental value of the frequency factor of the rate constant κ_∞ at 888°K is 8.10^{11} sec^{-1}, and this can be reasonably interpreted within the framework of any of the models considered above.

Gill and Laidler [66] used the classical theory of unimolecular reactions to evaluate the rate constant at intermediate pres-sures, although the condition of applicability of this theory $(\hbar\omega_i/kT \ll 1)$ is not fulfilled here (the characteristic tempera-tures, $\hbar\omega/k$, of the valency vibrations of N_2O are 1700 and 3000°K). They found that Slater's theory gives too low a value for the rate of activation and it cannot explain the observed pressure dependence of the decomposition rate. Kassel's theory, however, can be used to interpret the experimental data, if it is assumed that the effective number of oscillators, s_{eff}, is equal to 2 (instead of the actual number of vibrational degrees of freedom, $s = 4$). Since the mean lifetime of the active molecule for the quantized model is less than for the classical theory, it is obvious that Slater's theory will not yield the correct relationship between the reaction rate and the pressure even in the quantized case. Nikitin [15] has shown that a quantized statistical theory of decomposition can explain the experimental value for the decomposition rate of N_2O at low pressures, obtained by extrapolation of the experimental data to the desired pressure. It must be recalled here that the rate of activation by collision may be appreciably less than the number of gaskinetic collisions, because of the relatively large value of the vibrational quanta close to the reaction threshold (400–500 cm^{-1}). The low rate of activation does, in fact, imply that the interpretation of the rate of decomposition in the intermediate pressure range must be based on the mechanism of stepwise excitation, rather than on the mechanism of strong collisions. This means that the calculation of the probabilities of vibrational transitions on collision must take into account not only the possibility of the conversion of translational energy into vibrational energy, but, as was noted by Osipov [26], also the resonance transfer of vibrational energy between two N_2O molecules.

Finally, Wieder and Marcus [150] have calculated the rate of decomposition of N_2O within the framework of the quasi-equilibrium theory of unimolecular reactions. It was found that this theory does not give the correct explanation of the relationship between the rate constant and the pressure. Since this theory gives very satisfactory results for other reactions, it might be anticipated that the defect is due in this case to the nonfulfillment of one of the fundamental assumptions of the quasi-equilibrium theory—the assumption that the equilibrium rate of activation is conserved even under extremely nonequilibrium conditions (the strong collision mechanism). For adiabatic decomposition of molecules the mechanisms of stepwise excitation and strong collisions may not differ very greatly, since the adiabatic rupture of a bond always causes an appreciable decrease in the magnitude of the vibrational quanta of the active molecule in comparison with the vibrational quanta of the vibrationally unexcited molecule. It is this small magnitude of the vibrational quanta of the decomposing molecule close to the dissociation threshold that produces the relatively slight dependence of the probability of transition on the number of the vibrational levels, which, in turn, renders it impossible to make a clear distinction between the two types of activation.

Chapter III

THERMAL DECOMPOSITION OF DIATOMIC MOLECULES

13. THE EQUILIBRIUM THEORY OF DECOMPOSITION

Dissociation and recombination through an intermediate complex. If the vibrational energy of a diatomic molecule exceeds the dissociation energy, the molecule will decompose in a time of the order of the period of vibration (the only exceptions are the cases of nonadiabatic decomposition, when the probability factor may be appreciably less than unity). Since this time is considerably less than the time between successive collisions of the molecule, decomposition of the active molecule (in the sense of the definition given in Section 1) can always be assumed instantaneous and the observed reaction rate must always be determined by the rate of thermal excitation of the molecule to the dissociation limit. The earliest theories of the thermal decomposition of a diatomic molecule proposed by Rice [112, 113] and Careri [55, 56] were based on the assumption that the rate of thermal activation was the equilibrium rate. These two theories differed only in the relationship between the probability of dissociation and the vibrational energy of the molecule. Rice [113] and Widom [146] suggested that only those molecules AB* will become dissociated for which the vibrational energy lies in an energy interval kT close to the threshold energy. In this case the concentration of such molecules can be derived from the equations of the transition state theory, which give

$$[AB^*]/[AB] = \frac{F^*}{F} \exp(-\beta D). \qquad (13.1)$$

Here F is the total partition function of the molecule AB, F^* is the partition function of AB* and D is the dissociation energy of AB. In this expression the ratio F^*/F is greater than unity, since F^*_{vib}/F_{vib} is equal to the number of vibrational levels Δv in the interval kT, F^*_{rot} is larger than F_{rot} as a result of the large moment of inertia of the vibrationally excited molecule, and F^*_{el}/F_{el} is equal to the number of bonding electronic states converging to the dissociation limit.

The equilibrium rate of dissociation κ_{diss} can be obtained by multiplying Eq. (13.1) by the number of activating collisions which transfer the molecule from a region of the discrete energy spectrum (of width kT about the dissociation limit) into states with a continuous energy spectrum

$$\kappa_{diss} = Z\frac{F^*_T}{F} \exp(-\beta D) = A \exp(-\beta D). \qquad (13.2)$$

For the thermal decomposition of halogen molecules, the parameters which enter into the pre-exponential factor A have the following values: $F^*_{el}/F_{el} \approx 5$, $\Delta v \approx 10$, $F^*_{rot}/F_{rot} \approx 5$. Therefore, A may exceed Z by two orders of magnitude. The density of the vibrational levels for a hydrogen molecule is low ($\Delta v \approx 1$), but the effect of centrifugal extension is great ($F^*_{rot}/F_{rot} \approx 10$) and A may exceed the gas-kinetic number of collisions by an order of magnitude.

Thus Rice's theory formally explained the large values of A in the thermal decomposition rate constant which were obtained from the equilibrium constant using the experimental values of recombination rate constant.

Following the same method, Eq. (13.2) can be used to evaluate the recombination rate constant. This gives

$$\kappa_{\text{rec}} = ZF^* / F_A F_B, \qquad (13.3)$$

where F_A and F_B are the partition functions for the atoms A and B. If the explicit expressions for Z, F^*, F_A and F_B are substituted into Eq. (13.3), it becomes evident that κ_{rec} increases slightly with temperature. However, it has been found experimentally [50, 104, 105] that κ_{rec} for many reactions decreases sharply with temperature. Thus, Rice's theory is unable to explain the temperature dependence of κ_{rec}.

Realizing this shortcoming, Rice has proposed [114] another mechanism for the dissociation of diatomic molecules which proceeds via the formation of a weakly-associated complex of one of the atoms produced on decomposition with an inert molecule M

$$AB + M \underset{\kappa_2}{\overset{\kappa_1}{\rightleftarrows}} AB - M, \qquad (13.4)$$

$$AB - M \overset{\kappa}{\rightarrow} A + BM. \qquad (13.5)$$

It might be expected that the formation of the complex BM after dissociation would slightly lower the effective dissociation energy. Indeed, the rate constant of the overall process, corresponding to such a mechanism, can be expressed in the form

$$\kappa_{\text{diss}} = K_M \kappa, \quad K_M = \kappa_1/\kappa_2. \qquad (13.6)$$

It is, of course, essential that the concentration of the complex $AB - M$ is an equilibrium concentration and that this equilibrium

is not disturbed by the reaction (13.5), which represents the
unimolecular dissociation of the complex $AB - M$ along the $A - B$
bond. The rate constant for reaction (13.5) can, by assuming an
equilibrium rate of thermal activation (cf. Section 2), be calculated from Eq. (13.1), where F and F^* must be taken to denote the
partition functions of the complex $AB - M$ and of the active molecule $AB - M$, respectively; the effective dissociation energy of
the $A - B$ bond in the complex may differ slightly from the corresponding value in the free molecule AB. This difference is
apparently extremely slight [114], and will be neglected in the
following discussion. In the same approximation, the energy of
the bonds between the molecules AB and M and also between B
and M must be assumed identical. This fact makes it possible to
take the formation of the complex BM into account even in considering reaction (13.4). The following expression is then obtained:

$$\varkappa = \frac{F^*_{el}}{F_{el}} \, \widetilde{v} \, (r_m/r_e)^2 \exp\left(- \beta D\right). \qquad (13.7)$$

This expression is exactly analogous to Eqs. (3.6) and (6.2). The
multiplier $(r_m/r_e)^2$ takes into account the increase in the density
of the rotational states in the activated molecule $AB - M$ in comparison with the unexcited molecule. Here r_e refers to the equilibrium state of AB, and r_m is the mean interatomic distance in
the activated molecule (for which the corresponding position of
the representative point is on the peak of the centrifugal maximum).

The equilibrium constant K_M for reaction (13.4) can be evaluated by the usual statistical equations. In this case, in order to
emphasize its physical meaning, the constant can be conveniently
represented as the volume in configuration space which is

accessible to the stable molecule AB — M:

$$K_M = 4\pi a_0^2 \delta a \exp(\beta \varepsilon_M),\qquad(13.8)$$

where a_0 is equal to the effective mean distance between AB and M in the complex AB — M, and δa is the amplitude of the relative oscillations of AB and M. After substitution of Eqs. (13.7) and (13.8) into Eq. (13.6) it is found that the effective dissociation energy through the complex is less than the energy of the bond AB, which makes it possible to explain in principle the negative temperature dependence of κ_{rec}. Rice [114] and Porter [105] have investigated this possibility in detail and have concluded that the existing experimental data on the recombination of atoms at low temperatures (300-500°K) are satisfactorily explained by such a recombination mechanism.

The nature of the forces binding B and M is at the present time insufficiently understood; however, study of the relationship between κ_{rec} and the properties of the molecule M shows that they are definitely long-range forces. The energy of the bond BM, derived from the temperature dependence, changes for various recombining pairs and inert molecules M within the range of 0-4 kcal/mole [105, 122].

Obviously, such a reaction mechanism, via an intermediate complex, can be used for a direct calculation of the recombination rate constant for A and B. The limiting stage of this process will be the binary collision between A and the complex BM, whose concentrations can be determined from the equilibrium constant of the reaction

$$B + M \rightleftarrows BM.\qquad(13.9)$$

The number of binary collisions between A and BM depends on the nature of the interaction between the collision partners. For neutral molecules, the characteristic radii must be of the order of the gaskinetic collision radii; if one or both of the colliding particles are ions, the collision radii will be determined by the minimum impact parameter at which adhesion of A and BM will occur. On the basis of such a mechanism, Bunker and Davidson [50] calculated the rate constants for the recombination of the halogen atoms, and Fueno, Eyring and Ree [64] the rate constants for the recombination of ions, obtaining satisfactory agreement with the experimental values.

In calculating the equilibrium constant of reaction (13.4) or (13.9) it must be noted that the relatively simple expression (13.8) is valid only when the energy of the bond in the complex is large in comparison with kT. If $\varepsilon_M \lesssim kT$ the very concept of the complex becomes indefinite, and thus the calculation of its equilibrium concentration involves additional assumptions about the region of phase space which corresponds to complexes effectively participating in recombination. This arbitrariness, which leads to appreciable differences in the values obtained for $\varkappa_{rec}$, is connected with the incomplete understanding of the processes occurring in triple collisions.

It must be emphasized that the contribution of the dissociation mechanism via an intermediate complex decreases with temperature and becomes less important with a decrease in the polarizability and an increase in the ionization potential of the molecule M. The intermediate formation of a reaction complex on dissociation can not be used therefore to explain the negative temperature dependence of the pre-exponential factor of the rate constant for the decomposition of diatomic molecules at high temperatures. Under these conditions $(kT \gg \varepsilon_M)$, the theory of decomposition of diatomic molecules must be based on a thorough consideration of the mechansim of activating collisions, taking into account the possible disturbance of the equilibrium distribution of the vibrational states below the dissociation limit caused by the reaction. Although the difference between the mechanisms of strong activating collisions and stepwise activation may not be very great for the decomposition of complex molecules, in the case of diatomic molecules these mechanisms lead to basically different results.

14. A QUALITATIVE STUDY OF THE MECHANISM OF VIBRATIONAL EXCITATION OF DIATOMIC MOLECULES

In order to investigate the thermal activation of diatomic molecules it is essential to know the probabilities of transitions between the various vibrational states of the molecule AB, induced by collisions with M. In principle, this problem can be solved by calculating the cross sections of inelastic molecular collisions and then averaging over the velocities of the colliding molecules. It will be assumed henceforth that this averaging can be carried out using an equilibrium Maxwell distribution function. This assumption is based on the fact that in practically all experimental conditions the relaxation time for the translational degrees of freedom is much less than the characteristic time for energy exchange between the vibrational and translational degrees of freedom.

The quantum-mechanical, and even the classical problem of the excitation of vibrations on collision can be solved only for certain relatively simple models. These models can be classified into different types which are characterized by two dimensionless parameters η and ξ. The first parameter is proportional to the effective mean energy of interaction of AB and M which produces the excitation of AB on collision. For many models which have been more or less thoroughly investigated, the dimensionless parameter η can be set equal to the ratio of the amplitude of vibration of AB to the characteristic radius of action of the intermolecular force a. The second parameter ξ, which is known as the Massey parameter, is equal to $\Delta E a/\hbar v$, where v is the velocity of the colliding molecules and ΔE is the energy transferred on collision. The classical interpretation of this parameter can be obtained by replacing ΔE in the case of single quantum transitions by $\hbar\omega$, where ω is the frequency of vibration of AB. It will then become clear that ξ characterizes the time of the collision expressed in dimensionless units of the characteristic period of molecular vibrations as a scale. It follows from general considerations [8] that when the parameter ξ is large the collisions induce but a few transitions, causing merely an adiabatic displacement of the vibrational levels during the collision. The probability of transitions depends exponentially on ξ [cf. Eq. (7.22)].

The parameter ξ will now be evaluated for various collision conditions. In the case of single quantum transitions we set $\Delta E = \hbar\omega$, and assumed that the molecule AB can be satisfactorily represented by a Morse potential. In this case the frequency ω and the vibrational energy E of the molecule AB are connected by the expression

$$\omega = \alpha\left[\frac{2(D-E)}{m}\right]^{1/2}, \qquad (14.1)$$

where α is the Morse potential parameter (for the majority of diatomic molecules α is close to $2 \cdot 10^8 \, cm^{-1}$) and m is the reduced mass of AB. If it is also assumed that $v \approx (kT/\mu)^{1/2}$, where μ is the reduced mass of the system AB + M, it is found that

$$\xi = \frac{\Delta E a}{\hbar v} \sim \frac{\alpha a (D - E)^{1/2}}{(kT)^{1/2}} \left(\frac{\mu}{m}\right)^{1/2}. \tag{14.2}$$

This relationship can be used, for example, to evaluate the relative effect of short range (exchange) and long range (polarization) forces on the rate of vibrational excitation of the molecules. Since the characteristic dimension for the long range forces is the gaskinetic diameter R_0 which is at least several times greater than the radius of action of the exchange forces $1/\alpha$, it becomes evident that $\xi_{l.r.} > \xi_{exch.}$. Several-fold changes in the parameter ξ cause appreciable changes in the probability of transition if $\xi > 1$, since the probability depends exponentially on ξ. Thus when the collision velocities are low (so-called adiabatic collision) the effect of long range forces may be neglected.

In order to evaluate the Massey parameter for the excitation of the lower vibrational levels of diatomic molecules, only the short range forces will be taken into account. It will be assumed that $a\alpha \approx 1$ and $E \ll D$; this gives

$$\xi \approx \left(\frac{\mu}{m}\right)^{1/2} \left(\frac{D}{kT}\right)^{1/2} \tag{14.3}$$

For a gas consisting of molecules of approximately identical masses $(m \approx \mu)$ and at temperatures which are not too high $(D/kT \gg 1)$, ξ is appreciably greater than unity. This implies that vibrational excitation is in this case adiabatic, and that its probability is very low. It follows from Eq. (14.3) that the probability of vibrational excitation on adiabatic collision increases with temperature and with decreasing reduced mass of the colliding molecules. This relationship is described by the Landau-Teller equation (7.23).

If conditions are such that $\xi \ll 1$, the collisions will be of an extremely nonadiabatic nature. It is evident from Eq. (14.3) that such a situation can arise either on intense vibrational excitation $(D - E \approx kT)$ or on the vibrational excitation of a heavy diatomic gas by collision with molecules of a light gas $(\mu \ll m)$. The strong nonadiabatic condition $\xi \ll 1$ makes it possible to use a model with instantaneous collisions, such as, for example, the elastic-sphere model, in studying the relaxation and calculating the cross sections of inelastic collisions. Indeed, the radius of action a must in this case be assumed to be very small, which will fulfill the inequality $\xi \ll 1$.

Approximate calculations of the probabilities of transition based on the imposition of certain restrictions on η and ξ, have been carried out by many authors [9, 27, 58a, 58b, 71, 136a]. These calculations will not be discussed here. It must be noted that at the present time there is apparently no satisfactory physical model by means of which the relationship between the probability of vibrational excitation and the parameters η and ξ can be studied over the entire range of values of η and ξ. Nevertheless, a number of investigations [37, 38, 96, 110, 128], by means of numerical calculations for certain simple models, have succeeded in explaining the fundamental characteristics of multiple-quantum excitation, which could not be found within the framework of perturbation theory.

15. NONADIABATIC TRANSITIONS BETWEEN ELECTRONIC STATES OF THE DISSOCIATING MOLECULE

The previous discussion shows that the calculation of the dissociation rate constant κ_{diss} must be based on the solution of a system of kinetic equations which describe transitions between all the states in the discrete spectrum of the diatomic molecule, and transitions from the discrete into the continuous spectrum. Even in the simplest case, when the molecule M is an inert gas atom and its electronic excitation may be neglected, the system is extremely complicated, if only because each state of a diatomic molecule is characterized by a set of three quantum numbers— the vibrational number v, the angular momentum j, and the electronic quantum number n. The problem is made even more difficult by the fact that no method is known at the present time for even an approximate calculation of the probabilities of transitions between states which differ in all three quantum numbers. Thus, it is necessary to make an approximate and in some cases even a qualitative estimate of the effect of electronic and rotational transitions on the kinetics of vibrational relaxation and dissociation. This can be done on the basis of the following physical considerations.

The rate of dissociation is determined by the rate of transition between vibrational levels, the energy of which E^*, is slightly less than the dissociation energy (cf. Section 17). Below this energy, the distribution of the vibrational levels of the decomposing molecule approaches a Boltzmann distribution. Consider an electronic term of an excited electronic state which tends asymptotically to the same dissociation limit as a term of the ground state. If the energy E_n, which corresponds to the minimum of the excited term, is appreciably less than E^*, it may be assumed that equilibrium between the lower vibrational levels of the excited electronic state and the excited vibrational levels of the electronic ground state will be maintained during the dissociation process by way of collisionally induced transitions. The rate of these transitions, which are analogous to transitions in the case of forced predissociation, will be determined by many factors, including the overlapping of the vibrational wave functions which are disturbed during the collision by the effect of the atom M. The precise evaluation of the probability of such transitions requires a knowledge of intermolecular interaction of AB and M when AB is in an excited electronic state, and at the present time very little is known about such interaction. If the distribution of the lower vibrational levels of the excited state and of the corresponding levels of the ground state is assumed to be the equilibrium distribution, the rate of transition between the states must be appreciably greater than the rate of dissociation. The ratio of these rates contains an exponential factor of the form $\exp{[\beta(E^* - E_n)]}$, which increases rapidly as $E^* - E_n$ increases. It may be concluded therefore that equilibrium will be established for terms with a deep potential energy minimum. The rate of dissociation from such states can then be calculated as for the ground state, and the contribution of dissociation from these states to the rate constant will be additive with a weight factor equal to the ratio of the degeneracy of the excited state to the degeneracy of the ground state. In addition, the inequality $\exp{(-\beta E_n)} \ll 1$ must be fulfilled; only in this case dissociation through the electronically excited state represents an alternative decomposition pathway, proceeding parallel to decomposition from the ground state. This condition is, for example, satisfied by the two lowest excited terms of oxygen, $^1\Delta_g$ and $^1\Sigma_g^+$, at temperature of up to several thousand degrees. The statistical weights of these states are 2 and 1, respectively. Since the statistical weight of the ground state $^3\Sigma_g^-$ is equal to 3, the contribution of the excited states causes an increase in the rate of decomposition by a factor of approximately two.

The fact that equilibrium is established between the electronic terms during dissociation does not, of course, imply that it is established within a time of the order of the vibrational relaxation time. Apparently in the case of oxygen [22] a Boltzmann distribution is established during vibrational relaxation in the lower vibrational levels of the ground state, from which slow transitions proceed to the vibrational levels of the states $^1\Delta_g$ and $^1\Sigma_g^+$.

The effect of nonequilibrium dissociation for the electronic terms which lie relatively close to the dissociation limit can be estimated in a similar fashion but with less certainty. On the one hand, the Boltzmann factor $\exp\,[\beta(E^* - E_n)]$ is of less importance in this case, but on the other hand, the probability of nonadiabatic transitions between such terms must be much greater than between lower terms. This is due to the fact that the highly excited terms and the ground state terms usually arise from different electronic configurations, the nature of which determines the details of the intermolecular interaction of AB and M. If this interaction differs greatly in these two states, as is possible in the case of different electronic configurations, it is quite probable that intersection of the electronic terms of AB will be induced by collision with M. However, it is well-known [8] that the presence of such an intersection greatly increases the probability of nonadiabatic transitions. It might therefore be expected that transitions between electronic states close to the dissociation boundary would proceed at a rate of the order of the frequency of collision between AB and M. If the excitation energy of these terms is less than the energy E^* which characterizes the slow stage of the decomposition process, the lower vibrational levels of the excited state will be populated similarly to the levels at the same energy in the unexcited electronic state. In this case the electronically excited states provide a further pathway for decomposition, and this will increase the rate of dissociation. If, however, the excitation energy is greater than E^*, equilibrium will not be established between the unexcited and excited electronic states and therefore the latter will not contribute to the total rate of dissociation. Examples of such highly excited states are the $^3\Delta_u$, $^3\Sigma_u^+$ and $^1\Sigma_u^-$ terms of the oxygen molecule, the bond energies of which are of the order of 1 ev. These terms arise in the excited configuration $\sigma_g^2 \pi_u^3 \pi_g^3$; the two lower excited terms and the ground state term arise from the configuration $\sigma_g^2 \pi_u^4 \pi_g^2$.

Thus, the contribution of electronically excited states may, very approximately, be taken into account by multiplying the rate constant of decomposition, calculated for the ground state, by g_{el}, which is equal to the ratio of the total statistical weight of the excited electronic states with excitation energies less than E^* to the statistical weight of the ground state. A condition for the use of this factor is that the rate of nonadiabatic transition between the ground and these excited electronic states must be greater than the rate of decomposition.

It should be recalled that the energy E^* is a function of temperature (cf. Section 17). This means that the multiplier g_{el} must introduce an additional negative temperature dependence into the pre-exponential factor A. This additional dependence must be particularly important at a temperature T defined by $E^*(T) \approx E_n$. The nature of the temperature dependence of E^* can only be explained in greater detail if the exact mechanism for non-adiabatic transitions is known. If it is assumed that $E^* \approx D - kT$, an appreciable decrease in the rate of dissociation of oxygen should be observed at temperatures of approximately 10,000°K.

16. ROTATION OF THE DISSOCIATING MOLECULE

Theoretical considerations and experimental data show that vibrational and rotational excitation of diatomic molecules proceed practically independently for low vibrational quantum numbers v [7, 71]. This does not mean, however, that rotation does not affect vibrational excitation. The rotational relaxation time is considerably less than the vibrational relaxation time, and thus the process of energy exchange between the translational and vibrational degrees of freedom can be studied by assuming an equilibrium distribution of the rotational states. As the vibrational quantum number v increases the probability of transition between vibrational levels increases and the distinction between the two types of transition becomes less and less justified. Therefore a calculation of the rate of dissociation, for which an investigation of the transitions between vibrationally highly excited levels is essential, must take into account simultaneous vibrational-rotational transitions. However, as a result of the difficulties mentioned above, a calculation of this type has not been carried out, and therefore we must resort to an approximate correction for the effect of rotation. The possibility of carrying out such an approximation is due to the fact that the rate of dissociation of the molecules caused by purely rotational excitation is many times less than the rate of dissociation via vibrationally excited states. It might therefore be assumed that the change in the angular momentum of the molecule AB caused by collision with M has incomparably less effect on the decomposition rate constant than the change in the vibrational quantum number. In the zero-order approximation it could then be assumed that on collision the quantum number j remains unchanged, so that the rate constant could be calculated by taking into account only the vibrational excitation of the molecule AB, whose potential, however, includes the centrifugal energy $\hbar^2 j(j+1)/2mr^2$.

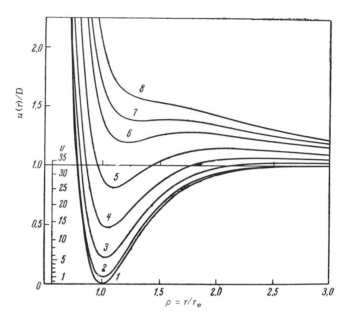

FIG. 6. Effective potential curves for the oxygen molecule. Curves 1–7 correspond to the values of j = 0, 40, 80, 120, 160, 200, and 220, and v_{max} = 33, 31, 25, 17, 9, 2, 0. Curve 8 corresponds to j = 240.

The above may be explained by using the oxygen molecule as an example. Figure 6 shows the effective potential curves of the oxygen molecule corresponding to various values of j as a function of the dimensionless interatomic distance ρ. It is easy to see that an increase in j causes a decrease in the effective dissociation energy, which is determined by the difference between the maximum and minimum values of the effective potential energy. However, the decrease in the effective dissociation energy δE is found to be less than the rotational energy of the molecule E_{rot}, and therefore, on averaging over all values of E_{rot}, the decrease in the population of the rotational states, described by a multiplier exp $(-\beta E_{rot})$, exceeds the exponential increase exp $(\beta\delta E)$ in the contribution of the excited rotational states to the rate constant. The result of the averaging indicates that the contribution of states with large values of j to the rate of dissociation is very small. This merely reflects the fact that the probability of the rupture of the A — B bond as a result of centrifugal extension is extremely small. Figure 7, taken from Bauer and Tsang [40], shows the energy regions corresponding to the bound and dissociated molecules expressed in the coordinates E_{vib}/D and E_{rot}/D. The heavy line represents the boundary between these regions, and the dashed lines represent constant total energy $E_{rot} + E_{vib}$. The arrows which cross the dissociation boundary represent various decomposition pathways, and the arrows which lie entirely within the region of the bound state correspond to various types of transitions on vibrational-rotational relaxation.

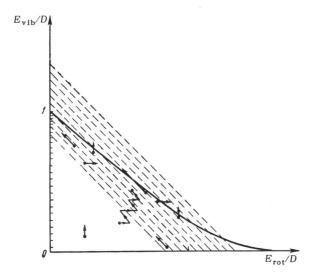

FIG. 7. The bound and dissociated states of diatomic molecules.

The approximation considered above implies that summation is carried out over all reaction pathways which are represented by straight lines parallel to the ordinate axis in Fig. 7. The result of such a summation can be formally expressed by introducing a multiplier g_{rot} into the expression for the decomposition rate constant calculated for a nonrotating molecule. It is clear that g_{rot} will depend relatively little on the temperature, and that g_{rot} is always greater than unity. Expressions will be derived below for g_{rot} for various types of potentials.

The following comments must be made in reference to Fig. 7. The calculation of the rate of dissociation as the rate of transition of the representative point through such a critical surface must take into account the distortion of this surface as a result of the interaction of AB and M. In the majority of theories dealing with the decomposition of diatomic molecules (see Section 17) interaction between AB and M is taken into account only in calculating the rate of vibrational activation, that is, the rate at which the dissociation limit is attained by moving along the ordinate axis; the dissociation limit itself is assumed to be independent of the interaction between AB and M. This approximation is only justified if the rate at which the boundary defining total dissociation is reached is determined by the rate at which the system traverses the reaction path, which in turn lies relatively far from the dissociation limit, so that displacements of the dissociation limit do not significantly affect the potential in the region of vibrational energies E^*. In connection with this the theory advanced by Light [89] must be mentioned. In this theory the rate of dissociation is related to the magnitude of the displacement of the boundary at the time of collision. Since, however, it is not possible by means of this theory to study the whole process of vibrational activation and thus establish the rate-determining stage of the decomposition, the theory cannot be used directly for the interpretation of experimental data.

Finally, we shall mention the approximations which are made in the simplest collisional theory for the calculation of κ_{diss}. The line which separates the dissociated and bound states is assumed to coincide with a line of constant total energy, which, however, is less than the total energy of the molecule by an amount equal to the relative kinetic energy of the molecules AB and M. The value which is obtained for A in this case is

$$A = Z (\beta D)^2/2. \tag{16.1}$$

The negative temperature dependence of the pre-exponential factor in Eq. (16.1) is due to the fact that the rotation of the molecule AB and the relative velocity of the colliding pair AB and M reduce the effective dissociation energy. In general, when the Hamiltonian of the system AB + M contains $2s$ terms which are quadratic functions of the momenta and of the coordinates and which contribute to the effective lowering of the dissociation energy, the temperature dependence of A may be expressed in the form $A = T^{1/2}T^{-s}$ [7]. Here, the multiplier $T^{1/2}$ is due to the temperature dependence of the number of gaskinetic collisions.

Equation (16.1) is obtained by integrating the Boltzmann distribution of the total energy E of the system AB+ M. Integration of exp $(-\beta E)$ from the dissociation energy to infinity gives a Boltzmann multiplier exp $(-\beta D)$ and a factor which is proportional to T. If the integration were limited to the energy interval $\Delta E \lesssim kT$, A would take the form:

$$A = Z (\beta D) (\beta D) (\Delta E \beta). \tag{16.2}$$

The pre-exponential factor in the rate constant given by Rice's equilibrium theory [113] is obtained from this expression if the effect of the translational degree of freedom of the relative motion of AB and M (the second multiplier) is neglected, if the contribution of rotation (the third multiplier) is given by the ratio $(r_m/r_e)^2$, and if it is assumed that $\Delta E \approx kT$.

In Light's theory, the effect of translational energy must be neglected, the effect of rotation is taken into account within the framework of the simplest collision theory, and ΔE, which is related to the displacement of the dissociation boundary, is assumed to be only slightly dependent on temperature. Light's theory [89] thus gives a temperature dependence for A of the type $T^{1/2}T^{-2}$. It must, however, be noted that a temperature law of this type is obtained only when the displacement of the dissociation boundary is determined by the average of localized interactions of AB and M and is independent of the relative velocity of the colliding molecules. It can be shown that this is equivalent to the assumption that the Massey parameter ξ is large. This, in turn, implies that the rate of vibrational excitation of the molecules must be very low (cf. Section 14) and thus the slow stage of the process will be vibrational excitation rather than transitions from the upper levels to the dissociated state, as was assumed by Light [89].

If the Hamiltonian of the system AB + M contains nonquadratic terms of the potential energy of AB, the temperature dependence of the multiplier A will differ from that given by Eq. (16.1). Light and Arnstein [90] have shown that if AB is represented by a Morse oscillator the temperature dependence of A is only slightly negative (less negative than $T^{-1/2}$), which is valid for a model of a truncated harmonic oscillator (a harmonic potential well of finite depth D).

17. MODEL CALCULATIONS OF THE DISSOCIATION RATE

Theoretical calculations of the nonequilibrium rate of dissociation of diatomic molecules which can be compared with experimental results deal mainly with the case of the decomposition of molecules in an atmosphere of a monatomic inert gas. The difference between the various calculations consists in the assumptions regarding the mechanism of energy exchange resulting from collisions of the atoms M with the vibrationally highly excited molecules AB. Since these assumptions lead to different types of temperature dependence for A, we shall consider the various theoretical mechanisms in greater detail.

Single-quantum stepwise excitation model. This model, which takes into account the relationship between the probability of vibrational transitions and the quantum number v, was first investigated by Nikitin [13] as well as Stupochenko and Osipov [29, 30]. These authors represented the nonrotating molecule as a Morse oscillator and approximated, in first order perturbation theory, the probability of transitions between vibrational levels in the collision of AB and M. The following qualitative picture of the distribution of the transition probabilities over the vibrational energy spectrum was obtained. In the lower region of the discrete spectrum transitions between neighboring levels only are allowed, and the transition probability increases rapidly with the vibrational quantum number. In the upper region of the spectrum transitions to nonneighboring levels can also occur. Finally, close to the dissociation boundary the probability of transition to the continuous spectrum becomes appreciable. The energy E^* which can be considered as the approximate boundary between the regions of single-quantum and multiple-quantum transitions can be determined from the equation [20, 26]:

$$\frac{\omega(E^*)\,a}{\bar{v}} \approx 1. \tag{17.1}$$

When $E \ll E^*$ the probability of vibrational excitation is given by the Landau-Teller equation (7.23). In this case the mean energy transfer $\langle \Delta E \rangle$ is very small, and it decreases exponentially as the vibrational quanta increase. When $E > E^*$ the condition $\omega a/\bar{v} \ll 1$ is fulfilled, vibrations of AB are unimportant during collision, and the mean energy transfer may be calculated within the framework of the impulse approximation [25, 27].

In order to calculate the rate of dissociation it is very important to know the region of the spectrum in which E^* lies. If E^* lies within a region of width kT close to the dissociation boundary, small changes in E^* within the limits of this region will not greatly affect the rate constant κ_{diss}. Indeed, although the rate of activation, characterized by the mean energy transferred $\langle \Delta E \rangle$, increases rapidly as a result of the effect of transitions between nonadjacent levels when $E > E^*$, this does not significantly affect the rate constant κ_{diss} which must always be less than the rate of activation of any one level. The rate of equilibrium dissociation from levels which are immediately adjacent to the dissociation limit can be expressed in the form $Z \exp(-\beta D)$. However, the rate of multistage vibrational excitation close to E^* can be approximately represented by an analogous expression $pZ \exp(-\beta E^*)$, where p denotes the probability of single-quantum excitation divided by the number of quanta in an energy interval kT below the level of E^*. The maximum effect of the final, rapid stage of the decomposition process can be estimated by decreasing the dissociation energy to E^*, then, because $D - E^* \ll kT$, the corresponding change in κ_{diss} will be small.

In cases where E^* is comparatively far from the dissociation limit, it is more difficult to make analogous estimates of the effect of various stages of the decomposition rate.

Consider the dissociation of molecules AB when the masses m and μ are approximately equal. Using a Morse oscillator as a model, it will be assumed that

$$\omega (E) = \alpha \left[\frac{2 (D - E)}{m} \right]^{1/2}, \quad \bar{v} \approx (kT/\mu)^{1/2}, \quad a\alpha \approx 1, \qquad (17.2)$$

whence it follows that

$$D - E^* \approx \frac{m}{\mu} kT. \qquad (17.3)$$

Thus the simplest case of the dissociation of molecules AB in an atmosphere of an inert monatomic gas M (whose atoms have approximately the same, or greater, mass than the molecules AB) approximately corresponds to a model in which the only allowed transitions are between the adjacent vibrational levels. The probability of dissociation from the final vibrational level is also assumed to be much greater than the probability of vibrational transitions.

For a nonrotating molecule and a single electronic state the system of kinetic equations which describes stepwise vibrational excitation and dissociation is of the following form:

$$\frac{dx_0}{dt} = Z\,[-P_{0,1}x_0 + P_{1,0}x_1]$$

$$\cdots \cdots \cdots \cdots \cdots \cdots \cdots \cdots \cdots \cdots \cdots \cdots$$

$$\frac{dx_\varkappa}{dt} = Z\,[P_{\varkappa-1,\,\varkappa}x_{\varkappa-1} - (P_{\varkappa,\,\varkappa-1} + P_{\varkappa,\,\varkappa+1})\,x_\varkappa + P_{\varkappa+1,\,\varkappa}x_{\varkappa+1}]. \qquad (17.4)$$

$$\cdots \cdots \cdots \cdots \cdots \cdots \cdots \cdots \cdots \cdots \cdots \cdots$$

$$\frac{dx_n}{dt} = Z\,[P_{n-1,\,n}x_{n-1} - (P_{n,\,n-1} + P_\infty)\,x_n],$$

where Z is the number of collisions of AB and M, $P_{\varkappa,\varkappa\pm1}$ is the probability of transition between the vibrational levels κ and $\kappa \pm 1$, and ZP_∞ is the rate of transition from the final bound state into the dissociated state.

In general, there are two possible approaches to the determination of the rate of decomposition on the basis of the system of equations (17.4). The first approach, which has been studied by Montroll and Shuler [97], Kim [82], and Widom [147], is based on the evaluation of the mean time $\bar{t}$ required for transition of the molecule from an initial state, characterized by a certain distribution $x_\kappa(0)$, into the dissociated state. The time $\bar{t}$ is identified by the reciprocal of the experimental decomposition rate constant κ_{diss}. This method is not completely satisfactory since in many cases it is impossible to separate the time scales of the processes of dissociation and vibrational relaxation, and thus the overall process cannot be described by a single constant κ_{diss}.*

The second approach [13, 20, 98] is based on an approximate solution of the system of equations (17.4). It is found that this approach makes it possible to understand the conditions under which the processes of relaxation and dissociation are separable and, in principle, to estimate the effects caused by their overlapping. This question will not be considered here; it will merely be noted that such a separation is possible when the rate of vibrational relaxation is appreciably greater than the rate of dissociation [9, 18]. A typical example is provided by the decomposition of molecules behind the front of a shock wave at such temperatures that the narrow zone in which there is a nonequilibrium vibrational distribution is followed by a wide zone of

---

*Ed. Note: The interference between these two time scales in itself, however, does not prevent one from computing $\bar{t}$, which is an independent observable. The mistake only comes in identifying such a $\bar{t}$ with the reciprocal of the rate constant.

nonequilibrium dissociation. Obviously, this does not mean that the system is characterized by a quasi-equilibrium vibrational distribution function for all the vibrational levels; the condition that vibrational relaxation is complete before dissociation commences implies only that the distribution function is close to the equilibrium function only for those states which are important for the mean vibrational energy of the molecules contributing to dissociation.

The expression for $\varkappa_{diss}$, which has been derived in a number of investigations [13, 20, 29, 30, 98] for constant temperature T has the form

$$\varkappa_{diss} = Z \left/ \left[\sum_{j=0}^{n} \exp\left(-\beta E_j\right) \sum_{\varkappa=j}^{n+1} \exp\left(\beta E_\varkappa\right)/P_{\varkappa,\,\varkappa-1}\right]\right. , \qquad (17.5)$$

where, for convenience of notation, it has been assumed that $\exp\left(\beta E_{n+1}\right)/P_{n+1,n} \equiv \exp\left(\beta E_n\right)/P_\infty$. (The case in which the temperature is variable, which can occur if the dissociation and relaxation overlap, will not be considered here [40, 70].)

Since the main contribution to the summation in Eq. (17.5) is due to the terms which correspond to vibrational levels close to the dissociation boundary, where $\beta\left(E_\varkappa - E_{\varkappa-1}\right) \ll 1$, the summation can be replaced by integration. Since the probability of single quantum transitions in the region $E \approx E^*$ is close to unity, the following expression is obtained for $\varkappa_{diss}$ [13, 30]:

$$\varkappa_{diss} = Z \frac{\hbar\omega}{(DkT)^{1/2}} \exp\left(-D/kT\right) \left[1 - \exp\left(-\hbar\omega/kT\right)\right]. \qquad (17.6)$$

Thus, for temperatures higher than the characteristic vibrational temperatures $\hbar\omega/k$ of the molecule AB, the pre-exponential multiplier A is inversely proportional to the temperature.

In order to explain the origin of the negative temperature dependence of A, Eq. (17.6) can be rewritten in the form

$$\kappa_{\text{diss}} = Z \frac{\langle \Delta E \rangle}{kT} \exp\left(-\beta D\right)/F, \tag{17.7}$$

where $\langle \Delta E \rangle$ denotes the mean energy transferred to a molecule AB close to the dissociation boundary in a single collision with M, and F is the vibrational partition function of AB. For the model under consideration $\langle \Delta E \rangle$ is determined by Eq. (17.1), that is, $\langle \Delta E \rangle \sim T^{1/2}$. In many cases the temperature dependence of A can be conveniently discussed on the basis of a formal evaluation of the recombination rate constant from the relationship

$$\kappa_{\text{diss}}/\kappa_{\text{rec}} = K, \tag{17.8}$$

where K is the equilibrium constant, which can be evaluated phenomenologically without an explicit investigation of the mechanism of energy transfer. The validity of Eq. (17.8) for the relationship between the nonequilibrium rate constants of dissociation and recombination will be discussed below (Section 18). The temperature dependence of the pre-exponential factor of the equilibrium constant is determined by the ratio of the partition functions for the relative translational motion of the dissociated pair A and B to that for the vibrational-rotational motion of the bound molecule AB. The former is proportional to $T^{3/2}$, and the latter to $TF(T)$. Since $Z \sim T^{1/2}$, Eqs. (17.7) and (17.8) give

$$\kappa_{\text{rec}} \approx \langle \Delta E \rangle/kT. \tag{17.9}$$

For the model of a nonrotating Morse oscillator this equation shows that $\kappa_{\text{rec}} \sim T^{-1/2}$. Rotation of the molecule and the presence of several electronic states can be taken into account approximately, in accordance with the discussion in Sections 15 and 16, by the introduction of a multiplier $g_{el} g_{rot}$ into Eqs. (17.6) and (17.7). Thus, the final expression for the decomposition rate constant is of the form

$$\kappa_{diss} = Z g_{el} g_{rot} \frac{\langle \Delta E \rangle}{kT} \exp\left(-D/kT\right)/F. \qquad (17.10)$$

Numerical evaluation of the multiplier g_{rot} for the dissociation of Br_2, on the assumption that the Morse formula for the interatomic potential is still valid close to the dissociation limit, shows that g_{rot} is practically independent of temperature and that its value lies approximately between 5 and 10 [13]. The factor g_{el} for Br_2 must be close to 5 and may be temperature dependent, thus producing a more negative temperature dependence for the pre-exponential factor than that given by Eq. (17.6). The temperature dependence of κ_{rec} derived from Eq. (17.9) is

$$\kappa_{rec} \approx g_{el} g_{rot} T^{-1/2}. \qquad (17.11)$$

In calculating the rate of dissociation from Eq. (17.10) it must be remembered that Z denotes the number of collisions with a vibrationally highly-excited molecule and this may be several times greater than the gaskinetic number of collisions between AB and M.

Single quantum stepwise deactivation model. Benson and Fueno [42] have considered a model of the recombination process in which deactivation during collisions of the vibrationally excited molecule AB with M proceeds by single quantum vibrational transitions. In evaluating a sum analogous to (17.5) these authors represented the functional dependence of the vibrational energy of AB on the number of vibrational levels by a quadratic function (this is justified for a Morse oscillator). However, in calculating the effect of rotation of the pair AB on the rate of recombination they took into account the long-range (polarization) part of the potential which is proportional to R^{-6}. The expression obtained for the recombination rate constant in one of the stable electronic states was

$$\kappa_{\text{rec}} = \lambda Z \left(\frac{1}{g}\right) \left(\frac{1}{\Delta v}\right) \frac{2}{3} \pi \langle r_m \rangle^3, \qquad (17.12)$$

where Δv is the number of vibrational levels of AB which lie in an energy interval κT about the dissociation boundary, Z is the number of collisions between AB and M, λ is the probability of single quantum deactivation, and $1/g$ is the probability of the electronic state of the molecule AB arising on the approach of A and B (for the atomic pairs 2H, 2N, 2Br and 2I, the values of $1/g$ for the electronic ground state are 1/4, 1/16, 1/16, and 1/16, respectively). The multiplier $2/3\pi\langle r_m \rangle^3$ is equal to the volume of configuration space which is accessible to the molecule AB close to the dissociation boundary; here $\langle r_m \rangle$ denotes the mean interatomic distance in that configuration of AB which corresponds to the maximum of the centrifugal potential barrier.

Benson and Fueno [42] and also Bunker [51] have derived the expression $\langle r_m \rangle^3 \sim T^{-1/2}$ for the temperature dependence of $\langle r_m \rangle$. In addition, it was suggested that the increase in the number of collisions Z with increasing temperature is largely compensated by a decrease in the effective collision cross section of AB and M. In this case κ_{rec} will be inversely proportional to T, and the dissociation rate constant calculated from Eq. (17.8) will contain one more multiplier $T^{-1/2}$ than Eq. (17.7).

In order to evaluate the probability multiplier λ in an explicit form certain assumptions must be made about the potentials of the interatomic interactions $A - M$ and $B - M$. Some qualitative information about these interactions can be obtained from data on the vibrational relaxation of the molecule. This approach has been used by Bauer and Salkoff [39, 123], who employed the same potential for the calculation of both the probability of transition between the lower vibrational levels of O_2 and the probability of recombination. These authors did not investigate multistage recombination although they concluded that recombination occurs principally as a result of the capture of the atoms in one of the highest vibrational levels of the bound state of O_2.

Finally, the work of Kretschmer and Petersen [85] must be mentioned. These authors calculated the recombination rate constant by evaluating $\langle \Delta E \rangle$ from Eq. (17.1). The result obtained from the temperature of $\varkappa_{rec}$ agreed with the conclusions of Benson and Fueno [42] (if the decrease in the collision cross section with increasing temperature is taken into account) or with expression (17.9) (if the collision cross section is assumed to remain constant).

Multiple-quantum stepwise excitation model. In evaluating the decomposition rate constant Rice [117] assumed that the mean energy transferred $\langle \Delta E \rangle$ is not determined by an equation of the type (17.1) but by the laws governing the collision of M with one of the atoms A or B of the molecule AB, each of which is considered to behave as a free atom. The following expression was obtained:

$$\langle \Delta E \rangle = \frac{4m_A m_M}{(m_A + m_M)^2} kT. \tag{17.13}$$

In deriving this equation it was assumed [117] that the main contribution to the exchange of energy during collision is due to those configurations of AB which correspond to the maximum extension of the A — B bond. Benson, Berend and Wu [43] have studied the classical interaction of an oscillator with an impinging atom in the impulse approximation and have shown that Eq. (17.13) is generally inaccurate; the energy transferred to the oscillator depends greatly on its vibrational energy, and not only on the relative energy of AB and M. If, however, Eq. (17.13) is accepted, as it usually is in simple theories of chemical reactions, then in the evaluation of the rate of decomposition, transitions between nonadjacent levels of AB must be taken into account. This is due to the fact that the value of $\langle \Delta E \rangle$ given by Eq. (17.13) is usually greater than the vibrational quantum spacing close to the dissociation limit.

An approximate estimate of the effect of multiple-quantum excitation can be made as follows. The rate constant of nonequilibrium decomposition is first calculated for single-stage excitation with an effective distance $\langle \Delta E \rangle$ between the levels. The expression obtained is then summed over all parallel reaction paths. This is equivalent to multiplying the expression by a coefficient g_{vib} which is equal to the number of vibrational levels in an energy interval $\langle \Delta E \rangle$ adjacent to the dissociation limit. For the model of a Morse oscillator, Rice obtained [117]:

$$g_{vib} = (\langle \Delta E \rangle D)^{1/2} / \hbar \omega, \qquad (17.14)$$

from which the following expression for the nonequilibrium dissociation rate constant is obtained:

$$\kappa_{diss} = Z g_{el} g_{vib} \exp(-\beta D) \left(\frac{r_m}{r_e} \right)^2 \frac{e^{-a}(1 - e^{-a})}{(1 + e^{-a})F}, \qquad (17.15)$$

where $a = \langle \Delta E \rangle / kT$.

If Eq. (17.15) is compared with the preceding formulas it will be noted that a is always less than unity, and therefore Eq. (17.15) may be rewritten with sufficient accuracy in the form

$$\kappa_{diss} = Z g_{el} g_{vib} \left(\frac{r_m}{r_e} \right)^2 \frac{\langle \Delta E \rangle}{kT} \exp(-D / kT) / 2F. \qquad (17.16)$$

Here, the multiplier $(r_m / r_e)^2$ replaces the coefficient g_{rot} of Eq. (17.10). The constant $\varkappa_{diss}$ for single-quantum excitation is obtained from Eq. (17.16) if it is assumed that $g_{vib} = 1$ and $\langle \Delta E \rangle \sim T^{1/2}$. For the Rice model $g_{vib} \sim T^{1/2}$, $\langle \Delta E \rangle \sim T$ and $r_m \sim T^{-1/4}$. In this case the use of Eq. (17.8) yields an expression for $\varkappa_{rec}$ in which the temperature dependence is represented by the function $g_{el}T^{-1/4}$. At high temperatures $(kT \gg \hbar\omega)$ the temperature dependence of the pre-exponential multiplier in Eq. (17.15) is $g_{el}T^{-1/2}$.

As noted above, multiple-quantum excitation may be particularly important in the dissociation of molecule AB in an atmosphere of an inert gas M when $\mu \ll m$. Bak and Lebowitz [36, 37] investigated in greater detail a model of such a process and found that A is proportional to $T^{-1/2}$ if rotation is not taken into account. In Rice's theory [117], for a nonrotating molecule and $g_{el} = 1$, the pre-exponential factor is independent of temperature. This difference is due to the fact that $\langle \Delta E \rangle$ is determined differently in the two theories.

Variational theory of decomposition reactions. It is clear from the above that the precise determination of the temperature dependence of the pre-exponential multiplier of the nonequilibrium decomposition rate constant requires a more detailed study of the interaction among the three atoms during collision. Even if the potential of this interaction were known, the problem could only be solved by the use of computers. For this reason studies of recombination cross sections are particularly promising—they involve the direct computation of the trajectories of the three atoms by the integration of the equations of motion using an electronic computer. Such computation also can select those trajectories which lead to the bound state of AB as a result of collision with M.

The promise of such an approach to the calculation of the recombination rate is due to the fact that, if the completion of a reaction is defined by the representative point in phase space intersecting a surface which separates reactants from products, then the problem can be formulated in terms of a variational principle. The difficulty will be quite clear if it is recalled that in general an imprecisely defined critical surface may be intersected several times by the representative point, and thus the condition that the critical surface is crossed is only a necessary (but not a sufficient) criterion for the reaction. Thus the direct determination of the number of trajectories which intersect in some definite manner the selected critical surface can provide a reasonable upper limit to the rate constant. This limit will gradually be lowered as the tentative critical surface is defined with greater and greater accuracy.

This method of calculating the recombination rate constant was first used by Wigner [151] who disregarded the effect of rotation of the pair AB on the recombination rate. The temperature dependence obtained for the upper limit of the rate constant κ_{rec} was $T^{-1/2}$. Recently, Keck [80] using the same method has taken into account the effect of rotation of AB and van der Waals interaction between M and the atoms A and B. The critical surface used in these calculations is shown in Fig. 8. Here $V_{12}(r_{12}) + J_{12}^2/2\mu_{12}r_{12}^2$ is the effective potential for the interaction between A and B (taking into account centrifugal energy); the distances between A and B, and between M and the center of mass of AB are plotted along the axes r_{12} and r_3, respectively; the total energy of the recombining atoms is plotted along the axis H_{12}. The tentative critical surface S consists of two planes S^A and S^B. The region of configuration space which lies between the potential energy surface and the planes S^A and S^B corresponds to the bound state of AB. The flux through S^A is given by the gaskinetic collision rate of AB with M; the flux through S^B gives the upper limit of the dissociation or recombination rate (depending on the direction of motion of the representative point).

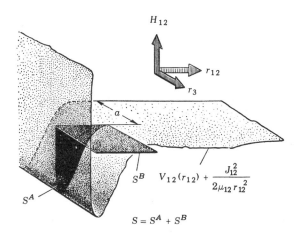

FIG. 8. Critical surface for the recombination of atoms.

It must be remembered that the constants κ_{rec} or κ_{diss} calculated in this manner will be larger than the true nonequilibrium rate constants. Consequently Wigner's method, which does not take into account the possibility of a multiple intersection of the critical surface by the representative point during a single three-body collision of A, B, and M, obviously will not take into account the crossing of the critical surface in the reverse direction as the result of a subsequent collision between a vibrationally highly-excited molecule AB and atom M. But it is this latter process (which is known as collisional redissociation) which causes the disturbance of the equilibrium distribution of the vibrational states of AB close to the dissociation threshold. This leads to a decrease in the nonequilibrium constants κ_{rec} or κ_{diss} relative to the equilibrium values. It follows that the constant κ_{rec} derived by Keck [80] should only be compared with the equilibrium rate constants of other theories, κ_{rec}^{equi}. In Rice's theory κ_{rec}^{equi} can be derived, for example, from Eq. (17.16), by omitting the factor $\langle \Delta E \rangle \beta$, which allows for the disturbance of the equilibrium distribution as the result of decomposition. Rice carried out such a comparison [117] and showed that Keck's theory gives a reasonable upper limit which, although very sensitive to the assumed shape of the interatomic interaction, can nevertheless be used for the evaluation of κ_{rec}. It is also essential in these considerations to take into account the possibility of the formation of electronically excited states of AB during recombination.

The variational calculation could be improved either by selecting a "better" critical surface, or by excluding from the calculation those trajectories which, as a result of a multiple intersection of the critical surface, return to that section of configuration space which corresponds to reactants. Since no method is presently known for the determination of the "best" surface, only the second method, involving the use of computer techniques, remains. Keck [81] has carried out such a calculation for the dissociation of a molecule AB, represented by a Morse oscillator, the interaction potential of AM and BM being described by a repulsive exponential function. The classical equations of motion for the six coordinates and six momenta which describe the relative motion of a triatomic system were integrated, and the obtained trajectories were classified in accordance with the number of times they intersected the surface $H_{12} = 0$. The result of a similar calculation is shown in

Fig. 9. Each three-body collision is characterized by two trajectories; the distance between the recombining atoms r_{12}, and the distance between M and the center of mass of the recombining pair r_3. The upper graph illustrates the collision $Ar + H + H$. The abscissa represents time in units of the periods of the small vibrations of H_2, and the ordinate represents r_{12} and r_3 in units of $1/\alpha$ (α is the Morse potential parameter, which for hydrogen is

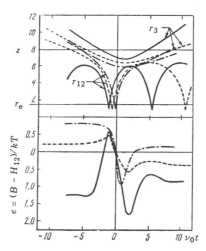

FIG. 9. Calculated classical trajectories of three atoms in collisions which lead to recombination.

equal to $1.93 \cdot 10^8$ cm^{-1}). The point z is the coordinate of the most probable position of the rotational barrier at a temperature T given by $kT/D = 0.01$. The solid lines represent the collision of Ar with a vibrationally excited H_2 molecule; the dash-dot line refers to the three-body collision $Ar + H + H$ without the formation of a bound molecule of H_2; and the dashed line represents three-body collisions leading to recombination. The lower graph shows the change in the relative energy of the recombining pair in a three-body collision. The ordinate is the dimensionless ratio of the difference between the energy of the rotational barrier and the energy of the pair H + H relative to kT. The three curves correspond to the three pairs of trajectories in the upper graph.

By statistical averaging over all the trajectories for which the initial state corresponds to the bound molecule AB + M and the final state to the dissociated molecule A + B + M, an expression can be derived for the dissociation cross section σ_{diss} as a function of the state of AB prior to collision, averaged over all energies of relative motion of AB and M. Keck [81] found the following relationship between σ_{diss} and the energy difference between the dissociation limit of the rotating molecule and its vibrational energy

$$\sigma_{diss} \approx (1 + \varepsilon)^{-3.5}; \quad \varepsilon = (B - H_{12})kT. \qquad (17.17)$$

This relationship is not sensitive to the mass of the atoms.

At present it is difficult to determine the extent to which this result may be considered as general, and how it would change if the interatomic potential were represented by a different function. The evaluation of the cross section σ_{diss} is one of the central problems of the theory of dissociation and recombination reactions, and the determination of σ_{diss}, even for a simple model within the limit of classical mechanics, is extremely important for the further development of the theory of elementary chemical reactions. The determination of the effect of disturbing the equilibrium distribution as the result of dissociation or recombination is a statistical problem which, however, cannot be solved without a preliminary determination of the cross section. The actual form of the cross section depends on the dynamics of the collision of AB with M.

Comparison with experimental data. Comparison of the above theories of the nonequilibrium thermal decomposition rate of diatomic molecules with experimental results can, of course, be carried out only at high temperatures when the effect of dissociation via the formation of an intermediate complex is known to be small (see Section 13). The majority of experiments on dissociation in shock tubes satisfy this criterion, and recently experiments have been carried out to determine the dissociation rate constants for Br_2 [101], I_2 [47], Cl_2 [76, 62], and O_2 [10, 54], in the temperature range 1000-8000°K. In all cases a negative temperature dependence was observed for the pre-exponential factor A. (Such an interpretation of the experimental data is, of course, obtained only if the parameter D in the equations is replaced by the spectroscopic dissociation energy. The experimental data can often be approximately represented by the Arrhenius expression with a temperature-independent pre-exponential factor and an effective dissociation energy less than the spectroscopic value.) The theory of single-quantum stepwise excitation gives a temperature dependence for A of the form T^{-1}, if the possibility of a nonequilibrium distribution in the electronic states of the dissociating molecule is not taken into account. The experimetal temperature dependence of A is often more negative; if for Br_2 dissociating in an argon atmosphere $A \sim T^{-3/2}$, then A for Cl_2 is proportional to $T^{-5/2}$. This divergence between theory and experiment is apparently due to the disturbance of the equilibrium distribution in the electronic states, which at present has not been taken into account in an explicit form, and, possibly, may also be due to the decrease in the effective collision cross section at higher temperatures. Nevertheless, evaluations of the absolute value of the rate of decomposition carried out for a series of molecules on the basis of the model of stepwise excitation [16, 98], give values which are sufficiently close to the experimental values.

If the dissociation of the molecule AB is investigated under a series of conditions associated with different values of E^*, which determines the slowest stage of the reaction, the corresponding values of the decomposition rate will differ. This is caused by the fact that the effective dissociation energy is not the energy of the bond AB but the energy E^* of the slowest stage. A decrease in E^* may be caused, for example, by the transfer of part of the internal energy of the molecule M to vibration of the dissociating molecule AB, which, to some extent reestablishes the disturbed equilibrium distribution over the vibrational levels of AB close to the dissociation boundary. This question has been discussed by a number of authors [17, 26, 72] for the transfer of rotational into vibrational energy and for the resonance exchange of vibrational energy during the collision. It has been shown in [17], for example, that the experimentally observed increase in the rate of dissociation of pure oxygen behind a shock wave front in comparison with the rate of dissociation of O_2 in an argon atmosphere can be explained by a mechanism of this type. If the equilibrium distribution were not disturbed during decomposition, the effect of the action of added Ar and O_2 should be almost identical, since the reduced masses and gaskinetic cross sections of the pairs $O_2 + Ar$ and $O_2 + O_2$ differ very little (in the experimental values of the rate constants at 4000°K differ by approximately one order of magnitude [53]).

18. THE NONEQUILIBRIUM DISTRIBUTION FUNCTION

The nonequilibrium distribution function x_k for thermal decomposition reactions can be determined from a system of equations of the type of (17.4). If the possibility of recombination is neglected, dissociation can be represented as a stochastic process of random walks of the molecules over the vibrational levels in the presence of a negative source (or an absorbing barrier) which acts on the upper levels. The length of step of the random walk, that is, the size of the energy jump which the dissociating molecule undergoes during collision with the inert molecule, depends on the accumulated vibrational energy of AB. The distribution of steps over the vibrational energy spectrum agrees qualitatively with the distribution of transition probabilities. Since the evaluation of the nonequilibrium distribution function depends on the solution of a comparatively complex system of equations, results can only be obtained for simple models. The main features of nonequilibrium decompositions will be discussed below, but without detailed considerations of the solution.

It should above all be noted that the system of equations (17.4) completely neglects the possibility of recombination. Although it is precisely this feature that makes a relatively simple solution of Eq. (17.4) possible, nevertheless this prevents an investigation of the process by which chemical equilibrium is established. In order to follow this approach to equilibrium, additional terms, which take into account recombination of the atoms A and B with the formation of a vibrationally excited molecule AB, must be introduced into the system (17.4). Of course, transitions also occur between nonadjacent levels but, for simplicity, only single quantum transitions will be considered and furthermore it will be assumed that dissociation and recombination only affect the highest vibrational level. In order to allow for recombination, the last equation in (17.4) must contain an additional term $\frac{1}{2} zp x_N$, where x_N is the concentration of the atoms and zp is the specific recombination rate (for simplicity it is assumed that A $=$ B). In addition the following equation must be added to the system:

$$\frac{dx_N}{dt} = 2ZP_\infty x_n - zpx_N^2. \qquad (18.1)$$

This equation corrects for the decrease in the concentration of the free atoms resulting from recombination.

The solution of such a system of equations in its general form is extremely difficult, since the last two equations are nonlinear. They can, however, be linearized if only the initial stages of the process are considered, for which either the change in concentration of the atoms Δx_N is small in comparison with the initial concentrations $x_N(0)$ or the effect of these concentration terms can be completely neglected. In this case the system of kinetic equations is of the form:

$$\frac{dx_\kappa}{dt} = Z\,[P_{\kappa-1,\,\kappa}x_{\kappa-1} - (P_{\kappa,\,\kappa-1} + P_{\kappa,\,\kappa+1})\,x_\kappa + P_{\kappa+1,\,\kappa}x_{\kappa+1}]$$

$$\cdots \cdots \cdots \cdots \cdots$$

$$\frac{dx_n}{dt} = ZP_{n-1,\,n}x_{n-1} - Z\,(P_\infty + P_{n,\,n-1})\,x_n + \frac{1}{2}\,zpx_N\,(0)\,y \qquad (18.2)$$

$$\frac{dy}{dt} = 4ZP_\infty x_n - 2zpx_N\,(0)\,y,$$

where it is assumed that $x_N^2 \approx x_N\,(0)\,[x_N\,(0) + 2\Delta x_N] = x_N\,(0)\,y$. The general solution of this system can be expressed in terms of the eigenvectors of the matrix B of the right hand side of Eq. (18.2):

$$\left.\begin{array}{c} x_\kappa \\ y \end{array}\right\} = \sum_\lambda A\,(\lambda)\,l_\kappa\,(\lambda)\exp\,(-\lambda t) \quad \text{when} \quad \begin{cases} \kappa = 0, 1, \ldots, n, \\ \kappa = N, \end{cases} \qquad (18.3)$$

where the summation is carried out over all the eigenvalues of the matrix B, and the coefficients are determined by the initial distribution $x_\kappa(0)$. The smallest (in absolute value) eigenvalue λ_0 is equal to zero, and the corresponding eigenvector $l_\kappa(0)$ gives the distribution function corresponding to total (that is, vibrational and chemical) equilibrium for a concentration of the atoms $x_N(0)$. If the next eigenvalue λ_1, is appreciably smaller than the remaining eigenvalues, it is possible to select a time interval Δt which satisfies the conditions

$$\lambda_1 \Delta t < 1,$$

$$\lambda_n \Delta t \gg 1, \ n > 1. \tag{18.4}$$

For times of the order of Δt the main contribution to the sum (18.3) will be due to the first two terms, and the condition which ensures the validity of the linear approximation will be fulfilled. All the remaining terms decrease rapidly with time. The physical meaning of the small value of λ_1 with respect to the remaining eigenvalues of the kinetic matrix B can easily be explained by noting that the next eigenvalue λ_2 corresponds to the rate of vibrational relaxation of the model system under consideration [21]. Actual calculations show [9, 13] that the condition $\lambda_1 \ll \lambda_2$ is fulfilled for many decomposition reactions over a wide range of temperatures. For example, for the dissociation of oxygen this condition ceases to be fulfilled at temperatures above 8000°K, which is experimentally observed as an overlapping of relaxation and dissociation processes [10, 54]. It follows from Eq. (18.3) that only when the inequality $\lambda_1 \ll \lambda_2$ is fulfilled it is possible to ascribe a definite value to the rate constant of a chemical process (dissociation or recombination).

The second eigenvector $l_\kappa(\lambda_1)$ of the matrix B gives the nonequilibrium vibrational distribution function. Since the matrix itself depends on the initial values of the concentrations $x_N(0)$, the form of the nonequilibrium distribution function will also depend on these concentrations. It will therefore be of interest to study some particular frequently encountered cases.

The initial stage of decomposition. If the conditions of the thermal decomposition are such that the chemical equilibrium of the reaction

$$AB \rightleftarrows A + B \qquad (18.5)$$

is greatly displaced toward the reaction products, and the initial state of the system corresponds to a totally undissociated gas (typical conditions for dissociation reactions studied in a shock tube), then in Eq. (18.2) it is possible to set $x_N(0) = 0$. This implies that the effect of recombination on the decomposition rate is neglected. It is by this approach that the problem of the evaluation of the rate constant (or, in other words, the evaluation of λ_1) has been solved in the majority of studies of nonequilibrium dissociation rates [13, 20, 21, 30, 37, 126, 129]. In this case decomposition is accompanied by an intense disturbance of the equilibrium distribution of the vibrational states of AB close to the dissociation boundary. Figure 10 shows the nonequilibrium distribution function $l_j(\mu_1)$, where μ_1 is the eigenvalue corresponding to this distribution function (obviously, $\mu_1 = \lambda_1$ when $x_N(0) = 0$). The explicit form of μ_1 for the single-quantum transition model is given by Eq. (17.5). The equilibrium rate of dissociation is obtained from Eq. (17.5) if it is assumed that the probability of transition from the highest vibrational level to the dissociation continuum is much less than the probability of transitions between the upper vibrational levels. In fact, this assumption is implicit in the equilibrium theory of dissociation reactions. However, in the majority of cases of practical interest the reverse relationship holds for these two probabilities [20, 24, 27]. Thus, the slowest stage of the whole multiple-quantum process is vibrational excitation of AB close to the dissociation threshold. Expressions for μ_1 calculated for various models and taking the above fact into account are given in Section 17.

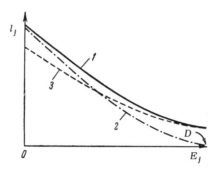

FIG. 10. Distribution functions characteristic of the dissociation of a diatomic molecule and that appropriate for the recombination of atoms. $1-l_j(0)$; $2-l_j(\mu_1)$; 3—the nonequilibrium distribution function resulting from recombination.

The approach to chemical equilibrium. In order to determine the characteristic time τ_{chem} required for a dissociation or recombination reaction to reach equilibrium, it is necessary to determine λ_1 assuming that the initial concentration of atoms $x_N(0)$ is equal to their equilibrium concentration. This calculation, carried out by Nikitin [21], gives

$$\lambda_1 = \mu_1 \left[1 + 4x_N(0)/K\right], \qquad (18.6)$$

where μ_1 is the rate constant for nonequilibrium dissociation, and K is the equilibrium constant for the reaction (18.5). Substituting $K = [A]^2_{\text{eq}}/[A_2]_{\text{eq}}$ leads to the expression

$$\tau_{\text{chem}} = \frac{1}{\mu_1}\left[1 + 4[A_2]_{\text{eq}}/[A]_{\text{eq}}\right]. \qquad (18.7)$$

The initial stage of recombination and the connection between the nonequilibrium constants $\varkappa_{\text{diss}}$ **and** $\varkappa_{\text{rec}}$**.** The rate constant of the initial stage of recombination, κ_{rec}, is obtained from Eq. (18.6) if it is assumed that $4x_N(0)/K \gg 1$. This constant describes the process of nonequilibrium recombination, which results in an overpopulation of the upper vibrational levels of the formed molecule AB, relative to the equilibrium distribution. In this case the possibility of redissociation from vibrationally highly excited levels, as investigated by Polanyi [102], has been taken into account. It can easily be seen from Eq. (18.6) that the rate constants for the initial stages of the recombination and dissociation process are related by the same expression as that which is commonly employed for processes which maintain the equilibrium distribution:

$$\kappa_{diss}/\kappa_{rec} = K. \qquad (18.8)$$

This multistage treatment of the processes of decomposition and recombination does, however, make it possible to determine the limits of validity of this expression, which are defined by the inequality $\lambda_1 \ll \lambda_2$. The meaning of this inequality for dissociation processes was discussed above. Applied to recombination it implies that all the relaxation processes must be completed before a noticeable decrease in the concentration of the atoms takes place. If it is assumed that κ_{rec} is of the order of magnitude of the three-body collision rate $z = Z_0^2 \tau$ (Z_0 is the binary collision rate per unit concentration and τ is the time required by a collision, of the order of 10^{-13} sec), and that λ_2 is equal to the rate of vibrational relaxation $Z_0 P_{1,0}$ ($P_{1,0}$ is the probability of the lowest single-quantum transition in AB), the condition $\lambda_1 \ll \lambda_2$ can be expressed in the form

$$Z_0 \tau [A] \ll P_{1,0}. \qquad (18.9)$$

By substituting here the values $Z_0 \approx 10^{11}$ liter $\cdot$ mole^{-1} $\cdot$ sec^{-1} and $P_{1,0} = 10^{-5}$ (the probability of vibrational deactivation for a molecule of the type of Cl_2 at $300\,°K$), it is found that the inequality (18.9) is fulfilled when $[A] < 10^{-3}$ mole/liter.

The nonequilibrium distribution function obtained as a result of recombination can be evaluated when $\lambda_1 \ll \lambda_2$ on the basis of the equilibrium distribution function as a linear combination of vectors $l_j(0)$ and $l_j(\mu_1)$. This function is shown in Fig. 10 (curve 3).

These two important conclusions of the theory of nonequilibrium decomposition rates—the range of validity of Eq. (18.8) and the relationship between the nonequilibrium distribution functions on dissociation and on recombination—are a consequence of the quasi-stationary nature of the reaction relative to other, more rapid relaxation processes. It is the uncertainty as to the precise limits of the applicability of these conclusions which has brought about the discussion of the validity of Eq. (18.8) [13, 20, 106, 116, 118, 148, 149].*

In using Eq. (18.8) it must be remembered that while the considered model allowed for the effect on the reaction rate of the disturbance of the equilibrium distribution of vibrational levels, it did not take into account the possible disturbance of the distribution of the electronic states of AB. To allow for this, the probability $P_{1,0}$ must be understood to represent the probability for the slowest (not necessarily vibrational) transition. In a series of cases the low transition probability from an excited

---

*It is often stated that for sufficiently large values of D/kT the equilibrium and nonequilibrium rate constants differ very little (see, for example, [58a]). This must be understood only in the sense that as D/kT increases, dissociation processes and relaxation processes can be separated with greater and greater precision. As for the population of the vibrational levels close to the dissociation limit, at any value of D/kT this population is appreciably less than the equilibrium population in the initial stage of dissociation, and therefore the rate of dissociation is always less than would be expected if an equilibrium distribution were maintained.

electronic state to the ground state can result in a violation of condition (18.9). The process of recombination, measured by the decrease in concentration of the atoms, will then be practically complete before stable molecules in the ground state are formed. The recombination of CO and O in a carbon monoxide flame is apparently an example of such a situation. The much-disputed cause of the "latent" energy of the CO flame [1] is, in all probability, related to the difficulty of transition from the metastable $^3\Pi_g$ state of the CO_2 molecule to the ground $^1\Sigma_g$ state. An analogous situation is, in principle, possible in the recombination of oxygen [29].

Experimental data which apparently clearly indicated the disturbance of the equilibrium distribution on recombination were first given by Christie [58], who investigated the recombination of iodine in various inert gases. Since the experimental conditions were such that it was impossible to exclude the recombination of iodine atoms by way of collisions with molecular iodine, the kinetic scheme must be represented in the form

$$I + I + M \rightarrow I_2 + M$$
$$I + I + I_2 \rightarrow I_2 + I_2. \tag{18.10}$$

It follows that the experimental recombination rate constant κ_{rec}^{exp} must be linearly related to the ratio $[I_2]/[M]$ (at a constant partial pressure of M). However, it was found that when this ratio is small the relationship is nonlinear (Fig. 11). This can only be explained by assuming that at small values of $[I_2]/[M]$ the slowest stage of recombination is some process which is not taken into account by Eq. (18.10). Christie [58] has proposed that the nonlinear nature of κ_{rec}^{exp} is related to a decreased probability for the vibrational deactivation of the newly formed molecule I_2^*, as a result of the decrease in the concentration of I_2.

This implies that the values of $\kappa_{rec}^{(1)}$ obtained by extrapolating (as $[I_2]/[M] \to 0$) the linear sections of the curves in Fig. 11 must be related to the recombination reaction $I + I$ in the presence of M with the provision that deactivation of I_2^* then proceeds by collisions with I_2. On the other hand, the extrapolation of the true curves must give a value $\kappa_{rec}^{(2)}$ for the recombination of $I + I$ and deactivation of I_2^* by collision with M. In the transitional region these two processes cannot be separated, and therefore Eq. (18.8) is not applicable.

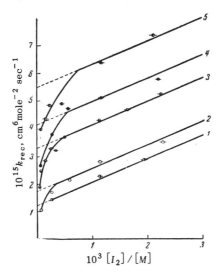

FIG. 11. Relationship between the recombination rate constants for iodine in various inert gases and the concentration of molecular iodine. Curves 1-5 are for M = He, Ne, Ar, Kr, and Xe; the points correspond to the experimental data of various authors.

Calculations carried out in connection with reactions (18.10) show that the interpretation of the slow stage as a process of vibrational relaxation is incorrect for recombination reactions under typical conditions as found in flash photolysis [21]. It must therefore be assumed that in the case of the recombination of iodine considered above the nonequilibrium process is related to the decreased probability of transition from the excited to the ground electronic state of I_2. The principal difference in the effectiveness of relaxation of I_2^* as a result of collisions with I_2 as compared to collisions with atoms of an inert gas is due to the fact that on formation of the complex $I_2^* - I_2$ the electronic terms of the combined system differ so much from the terms of two isolated iodine molecules that the probability of nonadiabatic transitions between those terms which approach each other closely in the complex $I_2^* - I_2$ is very large. In the interaction of I_2^* with an inert gas atom no large change in the position of the electronic terms is to be expected.

Chapter IV

THE DIFFUSIONAL THEORY OF CHEMICAL REACTIONS

19. THE CLASSICAL THEORY

The diffusional theory of chemical reactions, which was first formulated by Kramers [84] treats a chemical reaction as a process of diffusion of the representative point from the region in phase space which corresponds to the reactants into the region corresponding to the reaction products. The equation which represents the temporal development of the nonequilibrium distribution function $°x(\dot{q},q,t)$ can be separated into two parts. The first part is Liouville's equation, which can be expressed in the form

$$\frac{\partial x}{\partial t} + \dot{q}\,\frac{\partial x}{\partial q} - \frac{1}{m}\,\frac{\partial U}{\partial q}\,\frac{\partial x}{\partial \dot{q}} = 0. \tag{19.1}$$

Here $\dot{q}$ and q denote the velocity and coordinate of the representative point, respectively; and m is its mass. (For simplicity only the case of a single independent coordinate will be considered, although an analogous equation can be written for several variables.) The solution of this equation is the function $x(\dot{q}, q, t)$ which describes the mechanical development of a closed system as a function of time. In order to take into account the interaction of the reacting system with the surrounding medium (that is, with a so-called heat bath) the right hand side of Eq. (19.1) must contain terms which would primarily represent the diffusional transition of the representative point from one trajectory to another, and which would then lead to a Boltzmann equilibrium distribution function, $x^0(\dot{q}, q) = \exp [- \beta(m\dot{q}^2/2 + U(q))]$, for a stationary solution. It can be shown [32, 46, 84, 156] that in the simplest case these terms are of the form

$$b\dot{q} \frac{\partial x}{\partial \dot{q}} + bx + D\frac{\partial^2 x}{\partial \dot{q}^2} , \qquad (19.2)$$

where $D = b/m \beta$ is the "diffusion coefficient," and b, which is known as the "coefficient of viscosity," can be derived on the basis of certain assumptions about the interaction of the system with the heat bath. One of the basic assumptions, which is used in the derivation of the generalized Fokker–Planck equation

$$\frac{\partial x}{\partial t} + \dot{q} \frac{\partial x}{\partial q} - \frac{1}{m} \frac{\partial U}{\partial x} \frac{\partial x}{\partial \dot{q}} = b \frac{\partial}{\partial \dot{q}}(\dot{q}x) + D \frac{\partial^2 x}{\partial \dot{q}^2} , \qquad (19.3)$$

is that the period within which the distribution function changes appreciably is much greater than the characteristic fluctuation time of the heat bath. The validity of this assumption for various reactions will be considered below.

The first solution of Eq. (19.3) for the calculation of a reaction rate was obtained by Kramers [84]. He evaluated the reaction rate constant κ as the mean flux of particles across a potential barrier separating two regions of low potential energy, the density of particles in one region (corresponding to the reactants) being unity, and the density of particles in the second region (reaction products) being zero. The characteristic dimensionless parameter of this problem is the ratio of the viscosity coefficient b to the vibrational frequency ω_c, which characterizes the curvature of the potential barrier at its maximum. When the value of this ratio is large, during a transition across the potential barrier the representative point will undergo many activating and deactivating collisions with molecules of the heat bath and thus, in the region of the barrier, the distribution function will differ little from the equilibrium distribution. Consequently, the reaction rate must decrease as the ratio b/ω_c increases, since at equilibrium the net flux across the barrier is zero. A more detailed treatment gives [32, 46, 84]

$$\kappa = \nu_A \left(\frac{\omega_c}{b} \right) \exp\left(-\beta E_0\right), \qquad (19.4)$$

where ν_A is the frequency of small vibrations in the potential well of the reactants. At the present time it is unlikely that any reactions are known for which the condition $b/\omega_c \gg 1$ is fulfilled. Certainly, in the gas phase this condition is never fulfilled, since it implies that the frequency of intermolecular collisions is greater than the characteristic frequency of the intramolecular vibrations.

When the ratio b/ω_c is small the representative point scarcely interacts with the heat bath in crossing the potential barrier. This implies that almost all the molecules with energies sufficient to reach the peak of the potential barrier will cross over into the region of reaction products (it is assumed here and below that the transmission coefficient (see Section 6) is equal to unity). The rate constant can then be expressed in the form

$$\kappa = \nu_A \exp\left(-\beta E_0\right). \qquad (19.5)$$

This formula is exactly analogous to Eqs. (3.6) and (6.2) and consequently it corresponds to a unimolecular reaction at high pressures. As was noted above (see Section 6) it can be derived within the limits of the transition state method by averaging the flux over all the momenta and coordinates of a reacting system which is characterized by an equilibrium distribution function. In this case integration of the velocities is carried out for only one direction of the particle flux—the direction that leads to the reaction products. The approximations implicit in this approach can be better understood from a study of the nonequilibrium distribution function, found from Eq. (19.3), when the "viscosity" is low ($b/\omega_c \ll 1$). The general form of the nonequilibrium distribution function close to the barrier is [32]

$$x = C \exp\left[-\beta\left(\frac{m\dot{q}^2}{2} - \frac{m\omega_c^2}{2}(\Delta q)^2\right)\right] \times$$
$$\times \left(\frac{a-b}{2\pi D}\right)^{1/2} \int_{-\infty}^{\zeta} \exp\left[-(a-b)\zeta^2/2D\right] d\zeta, \tag{19.6}$$

where C is a normalization constant, $a = (b^2/4 + \omega_c^2)^{1/2} + b/2$, $\Delta q = q - q_c$, and ζ is related to q and q by the expression $\zeta = \dot{q} - a\Delta q$.

As the ratio b/ω_c decreases the integrand in Eq. (19.6) tends toward the δ-function, and thus, in the limit, phase space can be divided into three regions in which $x(\dot{q}, q)$ has three different forms: the first is the region of the reactants in which $E < E_0$, and where x is given by the equilibrium distribution x°; the second is the region of reaction products in which $E < E_0$, and where $x = 0$; the third region is the whole of the configuration space of the coordinate q for energies E greater than E_0. In the latter region the distribution function has a Maxwell-Boltzmann form only for velocities directed toward the reaction products; for oppositely directed velocities it is equal to zero. It is this type of distribution function which justifies the basic assumption of the transition state theory; namely, that the activated complex Z in the direction of the reaction $X \rightarrow Z \rightarrow Y$ always decomposes to form Y and never to form X [31].

It is not difficult to understand why such a formulation of the reaction rate problem cannot lead to a reaction which is second order, in which case the reaction rate constant would be proportional to b. This is due to the fact that, however small the value of b (that is, however low the rate of activation), Kramer's theory assumes that the change in configuration of the reacting system during the characteristic fluctuation time of the heat bath is small. For gas reactions this time is of the order of the interval between consecutive collisions of the reacting molecule with molecules of the heat bath $1/Z$. For example, in the decomposition of diatomic molecules, dissociation of the active molecule will obviously occur before it undergoes a further collision. It is for this reason that under such conditions Eq. (19.3) becomes inapplicable for states with sufficient energy to cross the barrier. Regarding transitions between bound states, these can still be described, with the accepted approximation, by Eq. (19.3). Under these conditions the problem of dissociation can be reduced to the random walk problem if Kramer's boundary condition is replaced by a new condition—the condition that all the particles which reach the highest bound level are completely absorbed. Thus, the region of phase space in which the concept of diffusion of a representative point is not valid is excluded from consideration.

This approach to the calculation of the dissociation rate of diatomic molecules has been formulated in a number of recent investigations [34, 35, 36]. Since the coefficient b is assumed to be small it is convenient to express the Fokker-Planck equation in terms of the canonical variables J (the action variable) and α (the angular coordinate). Since the times of interest are usually much longer than the characteristic times of intramolecular motion, the equation can be expressed in terms of J alone by averaging with respect to the angular coordinate.

For the simplest model of a harmonic oscillator with a potential well of depth E_0 (i.e., a "truncated" harmonic oscillator) the Fokker-Planck equation, expressed in terms of the energy $\varepsilon = \omega J$, takes the form

$$\frac{\partial x}{\partial t} = b' \frac{\partial}{\partial \varepsilon}\left[\varepsilon\left(1 + \frac{\partial}{\beta \partial \varepsilon}\right) x\right]. \qquad (19.7)$$

Here, as a result of the change of variables, the viscosity b' differs from the value of b in Eq. (19.3). Calculations show that the nonequilibrium distribution function $x(\varepsilon)$, determined from Eq. (19.7) and corresponding to the decomposition rate constant κ, is proportional to the product $\exp(-\beta \varepsilon) F\left(-\frac{\kappa}{b'}, 1, \beta\varepsilon\right)$, where F denotes a degenerate hypergeometric function. For large values of $\beta\varepsilon$ the function F can be represented approximately by an asymptotic function, which gives

$$x(\varepsilon) = \exp(-\beta\varepsilon)\left[1 - \frac{\kappa}{b'}\exp(\beta\varepsilon)/\beta\varepsilon\right]. \qquad (19.8)$$

From the condition $x(\varepsilon = E_0) = 0$ it follows that

$$\kappa = b'(\beta E_0)\exp(-\beta E_0). \qquad (19.9)$$

Since in the kinetics of gaseous systems b' is always proportional to Z, it is easy to see that the rate constant (19.9) is that of a second order decomposition, that is, it is analogous to the decomposition rate constant for diatomic molecules calculated in Section 17, or to the rate constant for the decomposition of polyatomic molecules at low pressures.

For the model of an anharmonic oscillator, the diffusional equation, analogous to Eq. (19.7), generally takes the form

$$\frac{\partial x}{\partial t} = Z \frac{\omega(\varepsilon)}{2} \frac{\partial}{\partial \varepsilon} \left[\frac{\beta \langle \Delta E^2 \rangle}{\omega(\varepsilon)} \left(1 + \frac{\partial}{\beta \partial \varepsilon} \right) x \right], \qquad (19.10)$$

where $\omega(\varepsilon)$ is the vibration frequency of the molecule AB in a state with vibrational energy ε, and $\langle \Delta E^2 \rangle$ is the mean square energy transferred to a molecule AB during collision with a molecule of the heat bath. It will be seen from Eq. (19.10) that the effect of anharmonicity on the rate of decomposition is associated with the relationship between the frequency ω and the vibrational energy ε. This relationship enters explicitly into Eq. (19.10) in the form of the function $\omega = \omega(\varepsilon)$, and implicitly in the term $\langle \Delta E^2 \rangle$, since the mean square of the transferred energy also depends on the frequency of vibration (see Section 14). Solutions of Eq. (19.10) for various models have been investigated by Bak and Andersen [34].

If decomposition of the molecules in excess of E_0 cannot be assumed to be instantaneous, a term must be introduced into the right hand side of Eq. (19.10) which takes into account the depletion of states with energies $\varepsilon > E_0$ as a result of decomposition. This term must obviously be of the form $-\kappa(\varepsilon)x$, where $\kappa(\varepsilon)$ is the rate constant of spontaneous decomposition from a state with an energy $\varepsilon > E_0$. The Fokker–Planck equation will then be valid for the dissociation of polyatomic molecules if the boundary condition $x(E_0) = 0$ is changed to the condition that $x(\varepsilon) \to 0$ as $\varepsilon \to \infty$ and if the function $\omega(\varepsilon)$ is redefined in such a way that, in the stationary case when $\kappa(\varepsilon) = 0$, a Boltzmann distribution function is obtained for the system of oscillators [18].

As was noted above (see Section 18) the rate constant of non-equilibrium dissociation κ_{diss} can be equated to the smallest eigenvalue of the operator which describes all the stages of relaxation and decomposition. In the case under consideration the corresponding equation is of the form

$$Z \frac{\omega(\varepsilon)}{2} \frac{\partial}{\partial \varepsilon} \left[\frac{\beta \langle \Delta E^2 \rangle}{\omega(\varepsilon)} \left(1 + \frac{\partial}{\beta \partial \varepsilon} \right) x \right] + \kappa(\varepsilon) x = \kappa_{\text{diss}} x. \qquad (19.11)$$

The variational principle can be used to evaluate κ_{diss}; applied to Eq. (19.11) this gives

$$\kappa_{\text{diss}} = \min \frac{\int \exp(-\beta\varepsilon) \left[Z \frac{1}{2} \langle \Delta E^2 \rangle \left(\frac{dy}{d\varepsilon} \right)^2 + k(\varepsilon) y^2 \right] \frac{d\varepsilon}{\omega(\varepsilon)}}{\int \exp(-\beta\varepsilon) y^2 \frac{d\varepsilon}{\omega(\varepsilon)}}. \qquad (19.12)$$

Here $y(\varepsilon)$ is any variational function which satisfies the boundary conditions $dy/d\varepsilon = 0$ when $\varepsilon = 0$ and $y \exp(-\beta\varepsilon) \to 0$ when $\varepsilon \to \infty$. For a system with many degrees of freedom $1/\omega(\varepsilon)$ must be equated to the density of the energy levels of this system. If the rate of decomposition $\kappa(\varepsilon)$ appreciably exceeds the rate of activation, the integral in the numerator of Eq. (19.12) will be minimum when $y(\varepsilon)$ is small for values of ε greater than E_0. It can be shown that the second term in the integrand is then much less than the first one. If the second term is neglected, the determination of the minimum of Eq. (19.12) reduces to the problem of the diffusion of a particle over the energy levels under the condition of total absorption at the level $\varepsilon = E_0$.

At the present time actual evaluations of the coefficient b' in Eq. (19.7) or (19.10) have been carried out for models involving single quantum transitions which occur as the result of atom-molecule collisions [12, 97], as well as for a model involving vibrational excitation of an oscillator as the result of interaction with an impinging light particle [36, 37].

For the first case, b' is given by

$$b' = Z P_{1,0} \hbar \omega \beta. \qquad (19.13)$$

Here $P_{1,0}$ is the probability of deactivation of the first vibrational level of the dissociating molecule. The fact that the classical constant b' contains $\hbar$ merely indicates that Eq. (19.7) is the classical limit of a quantized kinetic equation when $\hbar\omega\beta \ll 1$. The product $P_{1,0}\hbar\omega$ represents the mean energy of deactivation and has a clear classical meaning.

For the second case the calculations of Bak and Lebowitz [36, 37] give

$$b' = 4Ac\,(8\mu/\pi\beta)^{1/2}.\qquad\qquad(19.14)$$

Here μ is the mass of the atom impinging on the dissociating molecule, c is the concentration of atoms, and $2A$ is the effective cross section for a colinear collision.

It must be noted that the negative temperature dependence of the pre-exponential factor in expression (19.9) is a result of the disturbance of the equilibrium distribution of the vibrational states below the dissociation limit which, independently of the value of b', affects a region in the neighborhood of this limit of width kT. This type of disturbance of the distribution is not obtained from Kramer's theory.

It is interesting to observe that the diffusion equation (19.10) is valid for the description of the process of recombination of an electron and an ion A^+ in a three-body collision. Pitayevskiy has shown [28] that for a slightly ionized monatomic gas the rate of recombination is determined by the transition rate of electrons from those highly excited levels of the system $A^+ + e$ which have energy within kT of the dissociation limit, to lower levels. The use of a "molecular" model for the system $A^+ + e$, which makes it possible to carry out the averaging over the angular coordinate mentioned above, is possible only if the characteristic frequency of motion of the electron ω is much greater than the frequency of collision of $A^+ - e$ with A. In addition, if the collision time for the electron-atom interaction is appreciably less than $1/\omega$, then, in calculating the mean square of the energy transferred per unit time, the effect of the coulomb field can be neglected. In this case the following expression is obtained [28]:

$$Z \langle \Delta E \rangle^2 = \frac{128 \sqrt{2}}{3\pi} \frac{n\sigma}{\beta M} m^{1/2} |\varepsilon|^{3/2}, \qquad (19.15)$$

where m and M are the masses of the electron and atom, respectively, σ is the scattering cross section of a slow electron on an atom A, n is the concentration of atoms, and the (negative) energy ε is measured from the ionization boundary. For a coulomb field, the function $\omega(\varepsilon)$ is given by $\omega(\varepsilon) = C |\varepsilon|^{5/2}$; it will be seen from Eq. (19.10) that the value of C is unimportant. The validity of the "molecular" model and the momentum approximation imposes a limitation on the temperature which can be expressed in the form of an inequality:

$$e^2 n\sigma \, (m/M)^{1/2} \ll kT \ll (m/M)^{1/2} e^2/a, \qquad (19.16)$$

where a is of the order of the atomic dimensions.

20. THE QUANTUM MODEL

The classical diffusion theory of reactions can be quantized by taking into account the fact that the action variable J does not change continuously, but can only take on a series of discrete values. In this case, in place of the differential equation (19.7), an equation must be written in terms of finite differences. For the model of single-quantum transitions and for a value of b' selected in accordance with Eq. (19.13) this equation takes the form

$$\frac{dx_\kappa}{dt} = ZP_{1,0}\left[\kappa\alpha x_{\kappa-1} - [\kappa + (\kappa + 1)\alpha] x_\kappa + (\kappa + 1) x_{\kappa+1}\right]. \quad (20.1)$$

Here x_κ denotes the population of the κth vibrational level, and $\alpha = \exp(-\hbar\omega\beta)$. This equation has been used with the boundary condition $x_n = 0$ in a series of studies of the kinetics of overlapping relaxation and dissociation processes [12, 14, 57, 126, 127].

The explicit introduction of discrete transitions makes it possible to use Eq. (20.1) in studying a model of decomposition reactions in which the disturbance of the equilibrium distribution is determined not only by the total absorption of particles at the nth level, but also by the rate of this absorption. To do this it is sufficient to introduce into the final equation of the system (20.1), in place of the probability $\alpha P_{n-1,n}$, a new parameter P_∞. This parameter represents the transition probability from the highest discrete level to the dissociated state; the set of parameters $P_{\kappa-1,\kappa}$ (for $\kappa < n$) characterizes the process of vibrational relaxation. The rate constant for nonequilibrium decomposition, derived for this model, by Nikitin [14], is

$$\kappa = ZP_{1,0}(1-\alpha)\frac{P_\infty}{P_{1,0} + P_\infty/(1-\alpha)n}\exp[-\beta\hbar\omega n]. \quad (20.2)$$

The corresponding nonequilibrium distribution function has the form

$$x_\kappa = \exp(-\kappa\beta\hbar\omega)\left\{1 - \exp[\beta\hbar\omega(\kappa - n)]\frac{n}{\kappa}\frac{P_\infty}{P_\infty + P_{1,0}(1-\alpha)n}\right\}. \quad (20.3)$$

It will be seen from these equations that an intense disturbance of the equilibrium distribution occurs when the probability of transition to the dissociated state exceeds the probability of transitions between the upper vibrational levels, that is, when

$P_\infty \gg P_{1,0} (1 - \alpha)n$. In such a case the decomposition rate attains its maximum value (for a given value of $P_{1,0}$). As the rate of vibrational relaxation increases, that is, as the parameter $P_{1,0}$ increases, the rate of decomposition becomes larger. Expressions (20.2) and (20.3) become identical with Eqs. (19.9) and (19.8) when $P_\infty \gg P_{1,0} n$ and $\beta \hbar \omega \ll 1$.

It must be noted that the extension of the simplest diffusional theory and, in particular equation (19.7), to quantized systems does not necessarily lead to a model with single-quantum transitions. This is because the diffusion equation of the classical theory gives only an approximate description of the random walk of the representative point. In order to characterize the stochastic process more precisely an integral equation must be used [32]. The transformation from an integral equation to a differential equation is possible only under the condition that the ratio of the step-length of the random walk $\langle \Delta E \rangle$ to that integral of the energy $\tilde{E}$ which is of interest for the evaluation of the rate of decomposition be small. However, even if this condition is fulfilled such a transformation must be investigated very carefully, since it may happen that the ratio $\langle \Delta E \rangle / \tilde{E}$ does not serve as an adequate criterion for the validity of such a transformation. Model reactions for which the distribution function must be determined from an integral equation have been studied by Bak and Lebowitz [37] and also by Hoare [72].

For the dissociation of diatomic molecules, when the decomposition of the active molecule can be treated as instantaneous, the corresponding equation takes the form

$$\frac{\partial x (\varepsilon)}{\partial t} = \int_0^{E_0} [K (\varepsilon, \varepsilon') x (\varepsilon') - K (\varepsilon', \varepsilon) x (\varepsilon)] d\varepsilon' - x (\varepsilon) \int_{E_0}^{\infty} K (\varepsilon', \varepsilon) d\varepsilon'.$$

$$(20.4)$$

The term $K(\varepsilon, \varepsilon')$, which describes transitions $\varepsilon' \to \varepsilon$ between bound states of the dissociating molecule (for $\varepsilon', \varepsilon < E_0$) or between bound and dissociated states (for $\varepsilon > E_0$), satisfies the principle of detailed balancing

$$K(\varepsilon, \varepsilon') \exp(-\beta\varepsilon')/\omega(\varepsilon') = K(\varepsilon', \varepsilon) \exp(-\beta\varepsilon)/\omega(\varepsilon). \qquad (20.5)$$

The decomposition rate constant $\varkappa_{\text{diss}}$ is expressed in terms of the nonequilibrium distribution function $x(\varepsilon)$ which corresponds to the smallest eigenvalue of the operator of the right hand side of Eq. (20.4):

$$\varkappa_{\text{diss}} = \int_{E_0}^{\infty} d\varepsilon \int_0^{E_0} K(\varepsilon, \varepsilon')\, x(\varepsilon')\, d\varepsilon'. \qquad (20.6)$$

The approximations in the diffusional theory will now be considered which correspond to the various models for the mechanism of thermal activation considered above.

Strong activating collisions. In this case transitions between states of the dissociating molecule which are induced by the heat bath can cause a large change in the energy ε; therefore the Fokker–Planck equation is in principle inapplicable to the description of activation, and $\varkappa_{\text{diss}}$ must be determined from Eqs. (20.4) and (20.6). The approximation which employs the equilibrium rate of activation for nonequilibrium decomposition rates implies that the equilibrium distribution function can be substituted for $x(\varepsilon)$ in Eq. (20.6). A further simplification of collision theory is that the "active" degrees of freedom contributing to the rate constant of decomposition are treated as equiprobable.

Single-quantum stepwise excitation. Since transitions in this model are allowed only between adjacent states, $\varkappa_{\text{diss}}$ can be calculated from Eq. (19.12) under the condition $\hbar\omega/kT \ll 1$. By analogy with Eq. (19.8) a variation function is selected in the form $y(\varepsilon) = x(\varepsilon) \exp(\beta \varepsilon) = 1 - \exp[\beta(\varepsilon - E_0)]$ when $\varepsilon < E_0$, and $x = 0$ when $\varepsilon > E_0$. Since the integral in the numerator of Eq. (19.12) is determined mainly by terms close to the upper limit $\varepsilon = E_0$, and the integral in the denominator by terms close to the lower limit,

$$\varkappa_{diss} \approx Z \frac{\beta \langle \Delta E^2 \rangle}{\delta E} \exp(-\beta E_0) \beta \hbar \omega_0, \qquad (20.7)$$

where δE is some mean vibrational quantum spacing close to the dissociation limit. For single quantum transitions $\langle \Delta E^2 \rangle \approx (\delta E)^2$, and thus, in this case Eq. (20.7) coincides with Eq. (17.7).

Multiple-quantum stepwise excitation. In this case transitions close to the dissociation boundary are multiple-quantum transitions, but the effective energy transferred per collision is still sufficiently small and the Fokker-Planck equation remains valid. In Eq. (20.7) the substitution $\langle \Delta E^2 \rangle \approx (\delta E)^2 m^2$ must be made, where m is the mean number of quanta excited per collision. For this model, the mean energy transferred $\langle \Delta E \rangle$ is of the order of δEm. (This refers to the mean energy transferred during activation or deactivation, in accordance with the definition accepted in Section 17. The mean energy averaged over these two processes is always negative, since the effect of deactivation predominates, and has an absolute value of the order of $(\delta E)^2 m \beta$.)

Eliminating δE from these two relationships, the following expression is obtained from Eq. (20.7):

$$\varkappa_{diss} \approx Zm \langle \Delta E \rangle \beta \exp(-\beta E_0) \beta \hbar \omega_0. \qquad (20.8)$$

Since m must be set equal to g_{vib}, and g_{el} and g_{rot} are equal to unity, this expression coincides with Eq. (17.16).

If in the considered system transitions between nonadjacent levels are also important, and the step-length of the random walk is greater than kT, a complete system of kinetic equations of the type of Eq. (17.5)* must be solved. For certain particular cases a solution of the system can be obtained in an analytical form, but progress in this respect is apparently possible only by the use of computers. In this connection the investigations of Carrington [57] and Shuler and Weiss [129] on the calculation of the rates of relaxation and nonequilibrium decomposition for various models, must be mentioned.

Finally, quantum-mechanical variants of the diffusion theory of reactions which yield expressions of the type of (19.4) and (19.5) for the rate of decomposition must be discussed. For this case Kramer's model, studied in Section 19, will again be employed. The simplest quantum-mechanical variant of this model is for a tunneling transition of a representative point through a potential barrier separating two symmetrical potential wells. The condition under which formula (19.5) is then obtained is by assuming that in the region of configuration space (corresponding to reactants) the equilibrium distribution function holds with great precision, and during transit of the intermediate region on the way to produces (the peak of the potential barrier in the classical case, and the sub-barrier region for tunneling transitions) the heat bath has no effect on the system. But it was under exactly these conditions that Eq. (8.3), which gives the transition rate in the quantized version of Slater's theory, was derived earlier. Thus, the quantum analog of Eq. (19.5) in the diffusion theory is given by Eq. (8.3).

The limiting case of large "coefficients of viscosity" (for which, in the classical theory, Eq. (19.4) is valid) in the quantum

---

*Ed. Note: Equation (20.4) or a generalized version of Eq. (17.4) might be more appropriate here.

case corresponds to a strong interaction between the representative point and the heat bath during a tunneling transition. Since for heavy atoms the rate of tunneling transitions may be relatively small (appreciably less than the frequency of intermolecular collisions) this case may be of practical interest. The rate constant will here be proportional to the reciprocal of b, or to the number of collisions Z. This can be shown qualitatively as follows. Assume that each collision of a system undergoing tunneling transitions with a molecule of the heat bath produces a random distribution of the phases in the wave function which describes the nonstationary state of the system. In this case, after each collision the system will be localized in any of the potential wells. In the initial stages of the reaction it can be assumed that all the systems are in the potential well corresponding to reactants. If there were no interaction with the heat bath, the number of systems crossing from the potential well corresponding to reactants to that of products during a time t would be proportional to $\sin^2 (\frac{\Delta \omega t}{2})$, where $\Delta \omega$ is the vibrational frequency splitting close to the minimum of one of the wells as a result of the tunneling effect [8]. The approximation which assumes the "coefficient of viscosity" to be large implies that $\Delta \omega / Z \ll 1$. It is thus clear that the number of systems which cross the barrier during the time between consecutive collisions, $t \approx 1/Z$, will be proportional to $(\Delta \omega / Z)^2$. The number of systems crossing the barrier per unit time is obtained by multiplying this expression by Z. Thus, an expression of the type of Eq. (19.4) is obtained for the relationship between the rate constant and the pressure. This relationship (the rate constant is inversely proportional to the number of collisions) is extremely unusual for chemical kinetics and is due to the characteristics of tunneling transitions. It would be interesting to find a precise solution for the nonstationary problem which is based on a relaxation equation for the density matrix. At the present time this question remains completely unstudied.

REFERENCES

1. Gaydon, A. The Spectroscopy of Flames (Russian translation). Foreign Literature Press, 1959; Engl. ed. Wiley, N.Y., 1957.
2. Glasstone, S., K. Laidler, and H. Eyring. Theory of Rate Processes. Russian translation, Moscow, Foreign Literature Press, 1948; English edition, McGraw-Hill, 1941.
3. Gol'danskiy, V. I. Doklady Akademii Nauk SSSR, 124, 1037 (1959).
4. Gol'danskiy, V. I. Doklady Akademii Nauk SSSR, 124, 1261 (1959).
5. Gol'danskiy, V. L. Doklady Akademii Nauk SSSR, 127, 1243 (1959).
6. Kassel, L. S. Kinetics of Homogeneous Gas Reactions. Leningrad, ONTI, 1937; English edition, Chemical Catalog Co., New York, 1932.
7. Kondrat'yev, V. N. Chemical Kinetics of Gas Reactions. Russian edition, Moscow, USSR Acad. Sci. Press, 1958; English edition, Oxford, Pergamon Press, 1964.
8. Landau, L. D. and E. M. Lifshitz. Quantum Mechanics. Moscow-Leningrad, Fizmatgiz, 1963. Eng. ed. Pergamon, London, 1963.
9. Losev, S. A. and A. I. Osipov. Uspekhi fizicheskikh nauk, 74, 394 (1961).
10. Losev, S. A. and N. A. Generalov. Doklady Akademii Nauk SSSR, 141, 1072 (1961).
11. Mayants, L. S. Doklady Akademii Nauk SSSR, 151, 624 (1963).
12. Nikitin, E. E. Doklady Akademii Nauk SSSR, 116, 584 (1957).
13. Nikitin, E. E. Doklady Akademii Nauk SSSR, 119, 526 (1958).
14. Nikitin, E. E. Zhurnal Fizicheskoy Khimii, 33, 572 (1959).
15. Nikitin, E. E. Doklady Akademii Nauk SSSR, 129, 157 (1959).
16. Nikitin, E. E. Zhurnal Fizicheskoy Khimii, 33, 1893 (1959).

17. Nikitin, E. E. Doklady Akademii Nauk SSSR, 132, 395 (1960).
18. Nikitin, E. E. Doklady Akademii Nauk SSSR, 135, 1442 (1960).
19. Nikitin, E. E. Optika i spektroskopiya, 9, 16 (1960).
20. Nikitin, E. E. and N. D. Sokolov. Izvestiya Akademii Nauk SSSR, seriya fizicheskaya, 24, 996 (1960).
21. Nikitin, E. E. Kinetika i kataliz, 3, 830 (1962).
22. Nikitin, E. E. Fizicheskiye problemy spektroskopii, 1, 184 (1962).
23. Nikitin, E. E. Mol. Phys. (in press).
24. Osipov, A. I. Vestnik Moskovskogo Gosudarstvennogo Universiteta, 4, 97 (1958).
25. Osipov, A. I. and E. V. Stupochenko. Izvestiya Akademii Nauk SSSR, seriya fizicheskaya, 24, 992 (1960).
26. Osipov, A. I. Doklady Akademii Nauk SSSR, 137, 833 (1961).
27. Osipov, A. I. and E. V. Stupochenko. Uspekhi fizicheskikh nauk, 79, 81 (1963).
28. Pitayevskiy, L. P. Zhurnal Eksperimental'noy i Teoreticheskoy Fiziki, 42, 1326 (1962).
29. Stupochenko, E. V. and A. I. Osipov. Zhurnal fizicheskoy khimii, 32, 1673 (1958).
30. Stupochenko, E. V. and A. I. Osipov. Zhurnal fizicheskoy khimii, 33, 1526 (1959).
31. Temkin, M. I. Appendix 1 to N. N. Semenov's book "Some Problems of Chemical Kinetics and Reactivity." Moscow, USSR Acad. Sci. Press, 1958. Engl. ed. Pergamon, N. Y., 1958.
32. Chandrasekhar, S. Stochastic Problems in Physics and Astronomy. Moscow, Foreign Literature Press, 1947.
33. Shilov, A. E. Candidate's Dissertation, Institut khimicheskoy fiziki Akademii Nauk SSSR, 1955.
34. Bak, T. A. and K. Andersen. Technical Note, No. 4. University of Copenhagen, 1960.
35. Bak, T. A. and I. W. Plesner. Acta Chim. Scand., 14, 1310 (1960).
36. Bak, T. A. and J. L. Lebowitz. Disc. Faraday Soc., 33, 189 (1962).
37. Bak, T. A. and J. L. Lebowitz. Phys. Rev., 131, 1138 (1963).
38. Bartlett, M. S. and J. E. Moyal. Proc. Cambr. Phil. Soc., 45, 545 (1949).
39. Bauer, E. and M. Salkoff. J. Chem. Phys., 33, 1202 (1960).
40. Bauer, S. H. and S. C. Tsang. Phys. Fluids, 6, 182 (1963).
41. Bell, R. P. Trans. Faraday Soc., 55, 1 (1959).

42. Benson, S. W. and T. Fueno. J. Chem. Phys., 36, 1597 (1962).
43. Benson, S. W., G. C. Berend, and J. C. Wu. J. Chem. Phys., 38, 25 (1963).
44. Brabbs, T. A., F. E. Belles, and S. A. Zlatarich. J. Chem. Phys., 38, 1939 (1963).
45. Brauner, J. W. and D. J. Wilson. J. Phys. Chem., 67, 1134 (1963).
46. Brinkman, H. C. Physica, 22, 29, 149 (1956).
47. Britton, D., N. Davidson, and G. Schott. Disc. Faraday Soc., 17, 58 (1954).
48. Buff, F. P. and D. J. Wilson. J. Chem. Phys., 32, 677 (1960).
49. Buff, F. P. and D. J. Wilson. J. Am. Chem. Soc., 84, 4063 (1962).
50. Bunker, D. L. and N. Davidson. J. Am. Chem. Soc., 80, 5085, 5090 (1958).
51. Bunker, D. L. J. Chem. Phys., 32, 1001 (1960).
52. Bunker, D. L. J. Chem. Phys., 37, 393 (1962).
53. Camac, M., J. Camm, S. Feldmann, J. Keck, and C. Petty. Chemical relaxation in air, oxygen and nitrogen. Preprint No. 802. N. Y., JAS, 1958.
54. Camac, M. and A. Vaughan. J. Chem. Phys., 34, 460 (1961).
55. Careri, G. J. Chem. Phys., 21, 749 (1953).
56. Careri, G. Advances in Chemical Physics, 1, 119 (1958).
57. Carrington, T. Disc. Faraday Soc., 33, 44 (1962).
58. Christie, M. I. J. Am. Chem. Soc., 84, 4066 (1962).
58a. Clarke, J. F. and M. McChesney. The Dynamics of Real Gases. London, Butterworths, 1964.
58b. Cottrell, T. L. and J. C. McCoubrey. Molecular Energy Transfer in Gases. Butterworths, 1961.
59. Current, J. H. and B. S. Rabinovitch. J. Chem. Phys., 38, 783 (1963).
60. Current, J. H. and B. S. Rabinovitch. J. Chem. Phys., 38, 1967 (1963).
61. Cyvin, S. J. Spectrochim. Acta, 16, 1022 (1960).
62. Diesen, R. W. and W. J. Felmlee. J. Chem. Phys., 39, 2115 (1963).
63. Falconer, W. E., B. S. Rabinovitch, and R. J. Cvetanovic. J. Chem. Phys., 39, 40 (1963).
64. Fueno, T., H. Eyring, and T. Ree. Canad. J. Chem., 38, 1693 (1960).
65. Giddings, J. C. J. Chem. Phys., 22, 538 (1954).
66. Gill, E. K. and K. J. Laidler. Canad. J. Chem., 36, 1371 (1958).
67. Golike, R. C. and E. W. Schlag. J. Chem. Phys., 38, 1886 (1963).

68. Haarhoff, P. C. Mol. Phys., 6, 337 (1963).
69. Harrington, R. E., B. S. Rabinovitch, and H. M. Frey. J. Chem. Phys., 33, 1271 (1960).
70. Heims, S. P. J. Chem. Phys., 38, 603 (1963).
71. Herzfeld, K. F. and T. A. Litovitz. Absorption and Dispersion of Ultrasonic Waves. N. Y., Academic Press, 1959.
72. Hoare, M. R. Mol. Phys., 4, 465 (1961).
73. Hunt, G. R., E. F. McCoy, and G. I. Ross. Austr. J. Chem., 15, 591 (1962).
74. Hung, Ch. N. and D. J. Wilson. J. Phys. Chem., 66, 342 (1962).
75. Hung, Ch. N. and D. J. Wilson. J. Chem. Phys., 38, 828 (1963).
76. Jacobs, T. A. and R. R. Giedt. J. Chem. Phys., 39, 749 (1963).
77. Johnston, H. S. J. Chem. Phys., 19, 663 (1951).
78. Johnston, H. S. and D. Rapp. J. Am. Chem. Soc., 83, 1 (1961).
79. Kasha, M. Disc. Faraday Soc., 9, 14 (1950).
80. Keck, J. C. J. Chem. Phys., 32, 1035 (1960).
81. Keck, J. C. Disc. Faraday Soc., 33, 173 (1962).
82. Kim, S. K. J. Chem. Phys., 28, 1057 (1958).
83. Kohlmaier, G. H. and B. S. Rabinovitch. J. Chem. Phys., 38, 1692 (1963).
84. Kramers, H. A. Physica, 7, 24 (1940).
85. Kretschmer, C. B. and H. L. Petersen. J. Chem. Phys., 39, 1772 (1963).
86. Landau, L. Phys. Z. Sow., 10, 67 (1936).
87. Landau, L. and E. Teller. Phys. Z. Sow., 10, 34 (1936).
88. Levitt, B. P. Trans. Faraday Soc., 59, 59 (1963).
89. Light, J. C. J. Chem. Phys., 36, 1016 (1962).
90. Light, J. C. and R. Arnstein. J. Chem. Phys., 37, 2240 (1962).
90a. Lin, S. H. and H. Eyring. J. Chem. Phys., 39, 1577 (1963).
91. Magee, J. L., W. Shand, and H. Eyring. J. Am. Chem. Soc., 63, 677 (1941).
92. Mahan, B. H. J. Phys. Chem., 62, 100 (1958).
93. Marcus, R. A. and O. K. Rice. J. Phys. Coll. Chem., 55, 894 (1951).
94. Marcus, R. A. J. Chem. Phys., 20, 359, 364 (1952).
95. McCoy, E. F., S. S. Parfitt, and I. G. Ross. J. Chem. Phys., 64, 1079 (1960).
95a. Michel, K. W., H. A. Olschewski, H. Richtering, and H. G. Wagner. Z. Phys. Chem., 39, 129 (1963).
96. Mies, F. H. and K. E. Shuler. J. Chem. Phys., 37, 177 (1962).
97. Montroll, E. W. and K. E. Shuler. Advances in Chemical Physics, 1, 361 (1958).

98. Nikitin, E. E. and N. D. Sokolov. J. Chem. Phys., 31, 1371 (1959).
99. Nikitin, E. E. Mol. Phys., 7, 389 (1964).
100. Nikitin, E. E. Mol. Phys. (in press).
101. Palmer, H. B. and D. F. Horning. J. Chem. Phys., 26, 98 (1957).
102. Polanyi, J. C. J. Chem. Phys., 31, 1338 (1959).
103. Porter, G. and B. T. Connelly. J. Chem. Phys., 33, 81 (1960).
104. Porter, G. and J. A. Smith. Proc. Roy. Soc., A261, 28 (1961).
105. Porter, G. Disc. Faraday Soc., 33, 198 (1962).
106. Pritchard, H. O. J. Phys. Chem., 65, 504 (1961).
107. Rabinovitch, B. S. and R. W. Diesen. J. Chem. Phys., 30, 735 (1959).
108. Rabinovitch, B. S. and J. H. Current. Canad. J. Chem., 40, 557 (1962).
109. Rabinovitch, B. S., R. F. Kubin, and R. E. Harrington. J. Chem. Phys., 38, 405 (1963).
110. Rapp, D. and T. E. Sharp. J. Chem. Phys., 38, 2641 (1963).
111. Ree, T. S., T. Ree, H. Eyring, and T. Fueno. J. Chem. Phys., 36, 281 (1962).
112. Rice, O. K. J. Chem. Phys., 9, 258 (1941).
113. Rice, O. K. J. Chem. Phys., 21, 750 (1953).
114. Rice, O. K. Monatsh. Chem., 90, 330 (1959).
115. Rice, O. K. J. Phys. Chem., 65, 1588 (1961).
116. Rice, O. K. J. Phys. Chem., 65, 1972 (1961).
117. Rice, O. K. J. Phys. Chem., 67, 6 (1963).
118. Rice, O. K. J. Phys. Chem., 67, 1733 (1963).
119. Robinson, G. W. and R. P. Frosch. J. Chem. Phys., 38, 1187 (1963).
120. Rosenstock, H. M., M. B. Wallenstein, A. L. Wahrhaftig, and H. Eyring. Proc. Nat. Acad. Sci. U. S., 38, 667 (1952).
121. Rosenstock, H. M. and M. Krauss. Advances in Mass Spectr., 2, 251 (1963).
122. Russel, K. E. and J. Simons. Proc. Roy. Soc., A217, 271 (1953).
123. Salkoff, M. and E. Bauer. J. Chem. Phys., 30, 1614 (1959).
124. Schlag, E. W., B. S. Rabinovitch, and F. W. Schneider. J. Chem. Phys., 32, 1599 (1960).
125. Schlag, E. W. and R. A. Sandsmark. J. Chem. Phys., 37, 168 (1962).
125a. Schneider, F. W. and B. S. Rabinovitch. J. Am. Chem. Soc., 84, 4215 (1962).
126. Shuler, K. E. Seventh International Symposium on Combustion. Butterworths, 1958, p. 87.

127. Shuler, K. E. J. Chem. Phys., 31, 1375 (1959).
128. Shuler, K. E. J. Chem. Phys., 33, 1778 (1960).
129. Shuler, K. E. and G. H. Weiss. J. Chem. Phys., 38, 505 (1963).
130. Slater, N. B. Theory of unimolecular reactions. N. Y., Cornell University Press, 1959.
131. Slater, N. B. J. Phys. Chem., 64, 476 (1960).
132. Slater, N. B. J. Chem. Phys., 35, 445 (1961).
132a. Slater, N. B. J. Chem. Soc., 1961, 606.
133. Slater, N. B. The transition state. Spec. publication of the Chem. Soc., 1962, No. 16.
134. Stearn, A. E. and H. Eyring. J. Chem. Phys., 3, 778 (1936).
135. Steel, C. J. Chem. Phys., 31, 899 (1959).
136. Steel, C. and K. J. Laidler. J. Chem. Phys., 34, 1827 (1961).
136a. Takayanagi, K. Suppl. of the Progr. Theor. Phys., 25, 1 (1963).
137. Thiele, E. and D. J. Wilson. Canad. J. Chem., 37, 1035 (1959).
138. Thiele, E. and D. J. Wilson. J. Phys. Chem., 64, 473 (1960).
139. Thiele, E. and D. J. Wilson. J. Chem. Phys., 35, 1256 (1961).
140. Thiele, E. J. Chem. Phys., 36, 1466 (1962).
141. Thiele, E. J. Chem. Phys., 38, 1959 (1963).
141a. Thiele, E. J. Chem. Phys., 39, 3258 (1963).
142. Tredgold, R. H. Proc. Phys. Soc., A68, 920 (1955).
143. Vestal, M. L. and H. M. Rosenstock. J. Chem. Phys., 35, 2008 (1961).
144. Vestal, M., A. L. Wahrhaftig, and W. H. Johnston. J. Chem. Phys., 37, 1276 (1962).
145. Whitten, G. Z. and B. S. Rabinovitch. J. Chem. Phys., 38, 2466 (1963).
146. Widom, B. J. Chem. Phys., 31, 1027 (1959).
147. Widom, B. J. Chem. Phys., 31, 1387 (1959).
148. Widom, B. J. Chem. Phys., 34, 2050 (1961).
149. Widom, B. Advances in Chemical Physics, 5, 353 (1963).
150. Wieder, G. M. and R. A. Marcus. J. Chem. Phys., 37, 1835 (1962).
151. Wigner, E. P. J. Chem. Phys., 5, 720 (1937).
152. Wilson, D. J. J. Phys. Chem., 64, 323 (1960).
153. Wilson, D. J., B. Noble, and B. Lee. J. Chem. Phys., 34, 1392 (1961).
154. Wilson, D. J. J. Chem. Phys., 38, 1098 (1963).
155. Wolfsberg, M. J. Chem. Phys., 36, 1072 (1962).
156. Wood, J. L. and A. Suddaby. Trans. Faraday Soc., 53, 1437 (1957).

INDEX

Activated molecule, energy of 56
  mean interatomic distance in 84
Activating collisions, strong 141
Activation, stepwise 30
  thermal, equilibrium rate of 84
Active molecule 2
  entropy of 4
  hypervolume of 16
  lifetime of 56
Active oscillator 40
Airy functions 70
Amplitude factor 13
Anharmonicity 51
Arrhenius, equation of 43
Association, bimolecular 15, 51

Balance equations 28
Barrier, rotational 115
Boltzmann, distribution of 28
  multiplier 30
Bond, rupture of 24, 66

Collisional redissociation 113
Collisions, binary 85
  effective, number of 5, 28
  gaskinetic 28, 82
  molecular, inelastic 2
  randomness of 6
  triple 86
Complex, intermediate 81
Configuration, critical 43
Configuration space 3
Constant energy surface 7
Coordinates, atomic 3
  internal 3
  nuclear 65
  reaction 4
Critical surface, projection of 8

Deactivation, stepwise, model of 107
Decomposition, bimolecular 45
  equilibrium theory of 81
  initial stage of 122
  spontaneous 22, 38, 59
  thermal 1, 81
Decomposition reactions, variational
    theory of 111
Degrees of freedom 5
  active 16
  nonactive 16, 45
  partition functions of 57
  rotational 52
  vibrational 53
Density matrix, equilibrium 42
Detailed balancing, principle of 6, 28
Diffusion coefficient 130
Diffusional theory 129
Dissociating molecule, electronic states
    of 90
  rotation of 95
Dissociation, cross section of 116
  limit of 38
  thermal 1
Dissociation boundary, displacement of
    100
Distribution function 9
  equilibrium 20
  nonequilibrium 30, 33, 118
  quantum-mechanical 42

Electron impact 2, 50
Energy, activation 2
  critical 2, 27
  degenerate level of 31
  distribution of 4, 46
  excitation, permissible 52
  intramolecular, redistribution of 40
  spectrum of 17

Energy, threshold 51
Energy barrier 73
Energy levels, calculation of the density
    of 47
  quantization of 27
Energy transfer, intramolecular 3, 18
Ethyl bromide, decomposition of 34
Excitation, multiple-quantum, model of
    109
  single-quantum, model of 101
  stepwise 31
    model of 101, 109
  vibrational, probability of 102
Eyring, theory of 3

Factors, pre-exponential 19
Fermi resonance 17
Flash photolysis 127
Fluorescence spectrum 37
Fokker-Planck equation 130
Frequency factor, calculation of 5, 46
Frequency, mean 48
  vibrational 11

Gaussian distribution 42

Hamiltonian 6
Harmonic approximation 17, 43
Heat bath 39
Hybridization 62
Hypersurface 7

Interaction, anharmonic 36
  nonadiabatic 36
  radius of 35
Intermolecular distance 36
Intramolecular motion, quantization of
    25
Internal rotations, partition function of
    55
Iodine, recombination of 128
Ion impact 50
Ions, decomposition of 62
Isomerization 1
  thermal 19
Isotope effect 58
Isotopic substitution 74

Kassel, model of 61
    quantum-mechanical 26
  theory of 9

Landau, statistical theory of 4
Landau-Teller formula 35
Landau-Zener approximation 70
Lifetime, distribution of 13
  mean 8, 14
Light, theory of 98
Liouville, theorem of 7

Mass, reduced 35
Massey parameter 88
Maxwell-Boltzmann distribution 132
Molecular frequency 14
Molecular states, sum of 20
Molecule, activated 2
  active 2
  diatomic 81
Morse oscillator, model of 17
  nonrotating 106
Morse potential 88
Motion, intramolecular 3
Multiple-quantum excitation 90
Multiple-quantum mechanism 37

Nonadiabatic transitions, probability of
    71
Nonequilibrium constants 123
Normalization constant 132

One-dimensional model 71
Oscillator, anharmonic 9
  critical 10
  harmonic 9
Oscillators, dynamically coupled 18
  number of 14

Partition function, molecular 7
  total 21
Phase integral 6
Photoexcitation 2, 37
Potential, anharmonic 16
Potential curves, for oxygen 96
Potential well, double, splitting of 43
Potentials, types of 98
Predissociation, limit of 38
Probability multiplier 108

Quanta, excited, number of 61
Quantum model 138
Quantum number, rotational 54
Quantum oscillator 39
Quantum theory 25
  experimental verification of 74
Quasi-equilibrium theory 45, 63
Quasi-stationary concentration 31

Rate constant 11
  dimensionless 40
  reduced 11
Reaction coordinate 63
Reaction rate, constant of 6
  reduced 15
Reaction threshold 33
Reactions, nonadiabatic 65
  unimolecular, thermally induced 19
Recombination 81
  atomic, critical surface for 113
  mechanism of 85

Relaxation, time of   35
  vibrational-rotational   97
Representative point   7
  reflection of   23
Rice-Ramsperger-Kassel, theory of   4
Rice, theory of   81
Rotation, center of   70
  internal   54
  three-dimensional   23
Rotator   54

Single-quantum mechanism   37
Slater, harmonic model of   60
  model of   41
  theory of   12
Slow electron, scattering of   138
Small perturbation, theory of   19
Spectral characteristics   47
Spin, electronic   67
Spin-orbit interaction   66
State, nonactive   2
Statistical model   12
Statistical weight   10
  approximation of   30
Stochastic process, random walks   119
Strong activating collisions, mechanism of
  6, 26
Surface, critical   3, 41
System, ergodicity of   12

Term, multiplicity of   66
Thermal activation   22
Thermal decomposition, approximation
  of   50

Transition complex   2
Transition, inelastic   30
  nonadiabatic   69, 90
  probability of   27
  resonance   44
Transmission coefficient   23
Triplet state   44
Truncated harmonic oscillator, model of
  100
Tunnel effect   2
Tunneling correction   73
Tunneling process   41
Tunneling transitions   43

Unimolecular reaction, classical theory
  of   1
  quantum theory of   25

Variational principle   136
Velocity, relative   35
Vibration, antisymmetrical   18
  normal, coupling between strong and
    weak   38
  torsional   21
  zero-point, energy of   30
Vibrational excitation, mechanism of
  87
Vibrational levels, density of   46
Vibrational terms   35
Volumes, partial   48

Wave function   68
Wigner, distribution function of   44